Riding
&
Hiking
Trail

"FOUR MORE MILES"

Four more miles,
Four more miles,
Oh how we ride,
Oh how we ride,
We all run over the hills and dales,
We lost a couple of horse shoe nails
We've all been sitting on blistered tails,
For four more miles.

The above
song was composed by
the people who created
the trail across the
state of Michigan.
It is sung to the
tune of
"Three Blind Mice"

THE MICHIGAN RIDING & HIKING TRAIL

True stories of the creation of the trail
Maps of each day's trail
and
Stories about the seven horse races
from shore to shore
from 1985 to 1991

by *Rhoda Ritter*
foreword by *Sally Wilhelm*

illustrations by Karen Thumm

Printed in the United States
of America
by
The Leelanau Enterprise

ISBN 0-9651614-0-4

Additional copies of this book
may be ordered by sending $14.95 plus
$.90 tax (Michigan residents) plus $3.50
postage and handling to:

The River Outpost
269 Broomhead Rd.
Traverse City, MI 49686

*Riding a horse cross-country can be a wonderful experience,
but it can also be dangerous. It is recommended that there
be considerable training and conditioning for both
horse and rider before either attempts
such an endeavor.*

Printed in the United States of America
Text design by Rhoda Ritter

This book is dedicated to my father,
Byron Russell Lightfoot, who carried
me at a very young age to the barn
and placed me the back of his Percheron
mare. All his life he encouraged my love
of horses and nature.

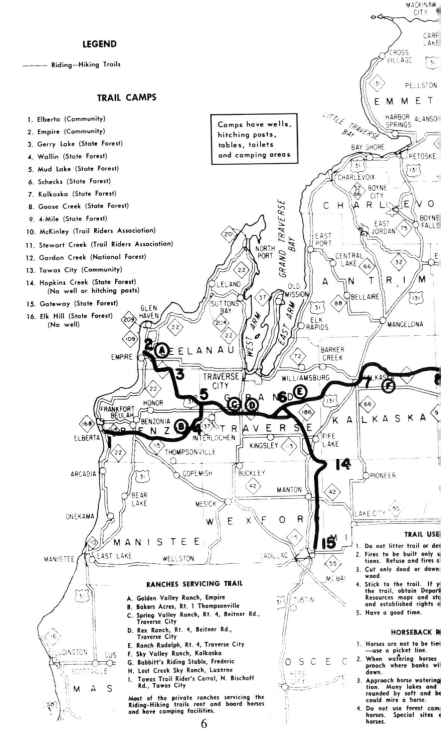

LEGEND

––––– Riding–Hiking Trails

TRAIL CAMPS

1. Elberta (Community)
2. Empire (Community)
3. Gerry Lake (State Forest)
4. Wallin (State Forest)
5. Mud Lake (State Forest)
6. Schecks (State Forest)
7. Kalkaska (State Forest)
8. Goose Creek (State Forest)
9. 4-Mile (State Forest)
10. McKinley (Trail Riders Association)
11. Stewart Creek (Trail Riders Association)
12. Gordon Creek (National Forest)
13. Tawas City (Community)
14. Hopkins Creek (State Forest)
    (No well or hitching posts)
15. Gateway (State Forest)
16. Elk Hill (State Forest)
    (No well)

Camps have wells, hitching posts, tables, toilets and camping areas

RANCHES SERVICING TRAIL

A. Golden Valley Ranch, Empire
B. Bakers Acres, Rt. 1 Thompsonville
C. Spring Valley Ranch, Rt. 4, Beitner Rd., Traverse City
D. Rex Ranch, Rt. 4, Beitner Rd., Traverse City
E. Ranch Rudolph, Rt. 4, Traverse City
F. Sky Valley Ranch, Kalkaska
G. Babbitt's Riding Stable, Frederic
H. Lost Creek Sky Ranch, Luzerne
I. Tawas Trail Rider's Corral, N. Bischoff Rd., Tawas City

Most of the private ranches servicing the Riding-Hiking trails rent and board horses and have camping facilities.

TRAIL USE

1. Do not litter trail or de...
2. Fires to be built only ... tions. Refuse and fires s...
3. Cut only dead or down... wood.
4. Stick to the trail. If y... the trail, obtain Depart... Resources maps and sto... and established rights ...
5. Have a good time.

HORSEBACK R...

1. Horses are not to be tie... —use a picket line.
2. When watering horses ... proach where banks s... down.
3. Approach horse watering... tion. Many lakes are ... rounded by soft and b... could mire a horse.
4. Do not use forest cam... horses. Special sites ... horses.

6

Michigan
Riding & Hiking
Trails

NORTHERN LOWER
PENINSULA

Trail Sign

Pump at Four Mile

TABLE OF CONTENTS

ILLUSTRATIONS

AUTHOR'S MESSAGE

I cannot remember how many times, while riding on this beautiful trail, that I have thought about Robert Frost's poem, "Into My Own". How he wishes he could steal away into the vastness of those dark trees, and never turn back. There is just something about sitting on a fine horse, with the flickering leaves protecting me from the harsh elements of the weather, going at a pace so slow and quiet I can sneak up on all kinds of wildlife in their natural surroundings, that is so good for the soul, the reasons for returning to the everyday ways of life are forgotten.

I moved to the Traverse City area in 1955, having been raised in Harbor Springs, on a farm where I was taught at an early age the love of horses by my father. By the time my oldest child was eight and the youngest was eighteen months, with a set of twins in the middle, we had a farm. Then came the horses, the first one being a childhood pet I had raised from a colt. Then came the trail riding.

We did our share of 4-H shows and fairs, but the real love was camping and trail riding.

We would visit the Wilhelm Department Store and caress the fine leathers. We bought our membership to the Michigan Trail Riders Association and treasured our pretty, yellow covered guide book with all the maps that showed us every mile of the trail from Empire to Tawas City. We rode to Shecks Place in 1964 from Acme. A route that should have taken us 3 hours (12 miles) took us 7. This is when we learned to keep the compass away from the steel in the saddle horn. We slept in tents and listened to the horses chew their hay, inbetween the calls of many whippoorwills, long into the night. The next day we played with our horses in the Boardman River before we started home. We were hooked.

Every June after that I tried to attend at least part of the June Ride. One rickety plywood, single axle trailer had to be jockeyed many times to accommodate all the kids I would take with me. I learned kids were just the best playmates; they wanted to go camping so bad, they were always on their best behavior.

I would get to witness the Wilhelms' and the Garns' having so much fun because they seemed to know everybody. They were always really nice to us and made us feel like they were glad we came to their ride.

As time wore on and the kids grew bigger, we could go longer. In 1972, we rode from Tawas City to Shecks Place with 6 teenagers in August. We had to jump our own rigs, and it was then we learned about reading maps and carrying compasses. How did Rex find it from camp to camp on those back roads without any road signs was a puzzle to us. We had many experiences, the many times we rode the trail and some of them are referred to throughout this book.

The kids grew up on the trail and we took up competitive trail riding. Parts of the trail were used for those events. It still is today. From 1985 to 1992, we sponsored the Shore to Shore Endurance Race which covered 50 miles a day in 5 days. People came from all over the United States and Canada to give it a try. I completed it four times. These stories are in the back of this book.

It is now 1995 and I am still riding the trail. My greatest place to explore is Elk Hill, which is also told about in this book. I have watched the organization grow, and the problems with the trail explode. In a world where we are slowly destroying our forests, I decided I had to do something to try to make people aware of the fact that we are very lucky to have such a wonderful place to ride our horses and hike in Michigan and somehow we must save it.

I have grown to know the people who created it and guarded it over the years. Some of them still ride it and some, because of health reasons or death, cannot anymore. Some have kept very good records of their experiences like Doc Lannen, and some of them have their experiences recorded in their heads. Evelyn and Bob Broegman have kept their memories via the many pictures all meticulously recorded and dated. Jean Lannen, Tony and Sally Wilhelm, Phyllis Garn, Bud and Barb Weaver, and Pat Worden have theirs recorded in their heads. Just one key word can bring out dozens of stories of incidents that we can all relate to from our own experiences. I wish to thank all of them and the many other people who have contributed to the history of the trail.

When I told them what I wanted to do, they were very helpful in getting me the information I needed to tell how it all began. They had fun together, and still do, but they worked hard making the trail all the way across the state, plus north and south from Cheboygan to Cadillac possible. They thought it was a nice idea if someone took the time to put it all down on paper for future generations to read about. Because of their humor and their willingness to share with you their stories, even if sometimes they were embarrassing, I think we managed to come up with a history that will be fun to read. Hopefully it will make you jealous you weren't there with them, but more hopefully, it will make you appreciate what they went through to carve that trail all the way across the state.

Today, the work, besides being laborious, is quite political, just trying to keep the trail. So much destruction has taken place in the woods since man entered into it, that the men whose jobs are to keep our forests natural seem to be fighting a losing battle. It is hard to designate a beautiful part of the forest for use, only to go back to find destruction and garbage. There are parts of it that make me want to vomit when I ride through the torn up hill, the wrecked mud bogs, and the dumped trash, sometimes whole households in one pile. The world is waking up to the fact that everything from the creepiest bug, to the thorniest bush, to the most beautiful song bird, are all part of the necessary world. I hope this book helps to save it.

Rhoda Ritter

ACKNOWLEDGMENTS

This book is really the creation of three women. One, being the author who you have already heard from; the other two are silent, but without them the book would've been undecorative and poorly composed.

Karen Thumm is a lady who lives on a beautiful river near Bellaire, Michigan. She grew up in Ann Arbor dreaming of horses. She now owns a quarter horse gelding. Her abilities to draw are limitless, but she loves to draw horses the best. Her upbringing and education taught her composition and graphics. She was a great help to me in making this book because she knows a lot of little secret ways to make things look right and she is such a perfectionist. The drawings at the heads of the chapters gave her a chance to make thoughts into pictures. The full page illustrations gave her the chance to express herself a little more, but the cover was what she can really do best. She, always critical of her own work, said it would never win any prises, but to me, it is a work of art. The maps at the beginning of each days ride on the trail were all drawn by hand. I would have been happy with just a copy of a county map, but she said they were too cluttered. I'm sure you will agree with me, that her art work really dresses up the book. Thank you Karen.

The other woman who you will not see any trace of in this book is the proof reader, Kathy Terrell. I swear she must have read some parts of it three or more times because I would keep adding things or changing them. She keeps her and her daughter's horses at my house and has ridden some of the trail when her health would allow her to ride. She is living with cancer and sometimes I think it would be better to say fighting with cancer. This disease is nasty and I have to give her credit for helping me even when she felt like just laying there and resting. She also proof reads for her husband who writes books about cross-country skiing and mountain biking. She says reading about riding on the trails helps her fight to get well so she can ride her horse with her daughter and go camping again. So, even though you don't see her corrections here, her presence is here and I am much obliged for her help. You know how it is when you write something and you wonder if it is written correctly. It's very comforting to get it right. Thank you Kathy.

FOREWORD

By Sally Wilhelm

      The year is 1995, and I am happy to see the story of the creation of the Michigan Riding and Hiking Trail being put on paper so that people can become aware that there is such a trail for them to use. It has been fun gathering the old clan together to tell the stories. Each story seemed to remind us of another. It made us remember the "old" days and all the good times we had riding our horses and camping in the northern Michigan woods. It made us remember "old" friends whom we had not thought of for years. The pictures different people had stored away in albums brought back memories similar to looking at an old high school year book.

      The people in this book shared many good times, and many challenges. We were all family people and the trail rides were formulated around that pattern. When we started remembering all the people who had helped through the years it made me realize how lucky we were to have had the opportunity to meet so many people with our same interests; a love of riding horseback through the woods.

      Our children had the chance to meet other children on a noncompetitive level and to grow up simply loving the outdoors and camping. It gave them an awareness of nature that only experiences can create.

      We did work hard making the trail, the signs, the bridges, the campsites, but the funny thing was we never thought of it as work. We formed the organization called the Michigan Trail Riders Association so we could get money and workers for the making of the trail. The Conservation Department and the U.S. Forest Service were very generous in helping make the trail a reality. Both governmental agencies sunk a lot of time and money into the trail and are still doing so. Many friendships were formed in those early days that have lasted through the years and they still have a special place in my heart.

      As you read through the book, please realize we were all friends and we loved to play jokes on each other. Like most horse people, we could have told enough more stories to fill ten books, but I think Rhoda has included enough to make it fun to read while learning how we went about getting from the shore of Lake Michigan to the shore of Lake Huron on horseback. We invite you to take your family and your horse and enjoy this wonderful trail.

PART ONE

THE GHOST RIDERS

As Rex Garn, Jim Hardy, Ernie Heim, and Harold Pence look down at the earth and focus in on the Michigan Riding Hiking Trail as it meanders across the state of Michigan, one end disappearing into Lake Michigan at Empire, and the other out into Lake Huron at Oscoda, they must be filled with pride and frustration. Pride, in that it grew to be used by so many, but frustrated because it requires so much time and money to keep it. The four might sit back on their logs around their campfire in the sky, and remember the good old days.

They all can still taste the delicious food cooked by Ernie and his wife, Evelyn. No fancy chuck wagon was used then - everything was cooked over a fire pit - except, that is, the wonderful breads and desserts created back at the Twin Lakes 4-H Lodge evenings.

Harold Pence and Rex Garn can remember being "unlost" by Jim Hardy and his forest service plane. When Jim had to pull fire watch and miss the rides - especially in the beginning when there wasn't a real pathway grooved into the earth - he would fly overhead and show them where to cross rivers, how to get out of the marked wood cuttings, and back on the trail.

Rex probably remembers those infamous words he heard in his delirium when he passed out at Goose Creek, "Rex, I don't know if you are well enough to hear me or not but you should know that you are being attended by three outstanding physicians in their respected fields, however, what ails you is not covered by our respective fields." He was left in a car behind a bar, and told not to drink or smoke until they got back with some drugs. He was sure glad to see those three guys come back.

Harold can probably remember riding with Jim when they first laid out the trail. The impossible bogs and dead ends he thought he never would get out of alive. Somehow Jim always found his way again. Harold can also recall the day he was riding with Tony and Sally Wilhelm through Death Valley and somehow got off the trail and ended up at a pile of junk. They knew they would have to ride back out the way they had just come in and it was lunch time. They decided this was as good a place to eat as any. While they were eating their lunch, a chain saw started up off in the woods. Harold made this remark; "Nothing like eating at a city dump listening to the sound of motor boats." Tony and Sally still remember that quote and when it is time to eat in the woods, they jokingly say that they have to find a city dump with motor boats in the distance.

These four men were among the sixteen who rode all the way across the state in 1964 on horses, starting on the beach in Empire and ending in the water of Lake Huron at Tawas City. Thirty-one years later, the membership of the organization they started numbers over 1500. Six different trail rides have to be scheduled to accommodate the numbers of people who want to ride a horse on their trail. How would you feel if it would've been your idea?

This book tells the story of the trials and the fun incurred by the people who made the Michigan riding and Hiking Trail across Michigan. It will also take you step by step across it yourself. Use it, have fun on it, and treasure it.

THE IDEA
Ch. 1

Do you know about the pathway that follows woodland trails and rivers from the lake shore on one side of Michigan to the other? If a person is seeking a peaceful escape from the sounds of civilization, and has a hankerin' for wild bird songs and small animal squeaks, he can find it by going either to Empire on the west side of Michigan, or Oscoda on the east and start following a pathway marked by small blue painted dots or a small trail marking sign with the ensignia of a horse's hoof print and a human foot print on the forest trees. For 250 miles he can meander along, walking or riding a horse, and find himself strictly among the nature of things.

The trail uses the natural things as much as possible by winding along rivers, and huddling up to little lakes so a traveler has a chance to use the water to cool himself if the weather takes a mind to be too warm, as Michigan is known to do in the summers. It also will surprise you with a serene camping spot, out in the middle of nowhere, with pit toilets and a hand pump with cool, fresh drinking water. If you are being carried by a horse, there will be posts set in the ground for you to tie him on a picket line if you care to spend the night. These campsites just happen to crop up about every 25 miles.

As the trail scuttles along, it will take you in close to little towns where there will be a store for supplies, a phone to call home and tell the folks you are all right, and usually the store keeper will be able to steer you in the direction of anything else you might need.

If you are not packing your gear on your back or a pack mule, you will need to get your supplies in by road. This is entirely possible. In fact, the modern age cowboy has a pickup truck with a camper, or a motor home with a horse trailer that accompanies him on his adventures. The campsites are large enough to fit in many of these rigs because this trail is used six times each summer by a group called the "Michigan Trail Riders Association". This group of urban cowboys migrates from the cities every summer and meets their friends at these campsites to spend many happy hours shuckin' and ridin' together. The MTRA, as it is called, sponsors these get togethers for people who love horses and nature, and guides them across the state from camp to camp. There is a trail boss who answers all the questions and keeps the pack in order. There is also a chuck wagon that provides some of the best food ever eaten. They move along from camp to camp like a giant wagon train making 25 miles a day, only in this case the horses take the pathway and the trucks with your gear have to go back out and take the highways. They leave the highways again at designated points that snake you back to the camps hidden in the woods.

Actually, this organization is the reason there is a trail, or maybe it's because of the trail, there is such an organization.

Let me tell you an interesting true story about how they both came to be what they are today:

It all started in the early 1960's. On the west side of the state there was a small group of people who loved to trail ride and camp with their families. Their names were Wilhelm, Garn, and Williams. On the east side was a dude ranch owner, named Jim Hardy, who flew fire watch for the forest service. One summer afternoon, the west side group was at a meeting on the east side and stopped in to visit the dude ranch. As Sally Wilhelm tells us, "We had gone to a meeting over in Mio and I mentioned to Tony that I'd like to visit the Lost Creek Sky Ranch, a ranch that I had been to before moving to Traverse City. It was west of Mio and I knew the lodge had burned a few years earlier. When we got there, we found a lovely new lodge and the new owner, Jim Hardy. We got to talking trail riding. He said he outfitted camping trips and he used a network of two track trails to get to Lake Huron and some that would get him to the Grayling area. We learned he was a pilot and he flew fire watch so he had a good way to find trails."

The idea of riding all the way across the state, from shore to shore, came into the discussion and sparked a fire. The more people they talked to the more the idea grew. So, the three families from the west and Jim Hardy took on the job of creating such a trail.

It was a labor of love because there was never a penny's profit made for all their time and energies. There were no big cash endowments, nor tax write-offs involved in the making of the trail. It was ordinary, hard working people, spending their own money, driving to meetings with the Department of Conservation and the Federal Forest Services to determine what trails could be used and what trails were on private lands.

Jim Hardy had a neighbor who worked for the Forest Service named Forest

Rhodes. He helped Jim set up the network of trails it would take to get from Tawas City to the Manistee River west of Frederick.

The group from the west lived just south of Traverse City. Rex and Phyllis Garn had a horse boarding and riding stable on the Boardman River. They had a son and a daughter who loved to ride horse. Fitch and Louise Williams had two daughters who rode. Fitch was a local attorney. Tony and Sally Wilhelm also had a son and a daughter who loved to ride. Tony managed the family department store in town.

Meetings were set up at various locations along the proposed route of the trail. Tony, Fitch, and Rex presented their ideas and they were met with considerable enthusiasm. Basil Smith, who had a barber business in the small town of Kalkaska got wind of the idea. He kept his horse in back of his barber shop in town. He was very helpful in spreading the word and helping to establish a camp in Kalkaska.

The history of Michigan lends itself to really benefit a trail riding organization. When the Pleistocene glaciers melted 10,000 to 16,000 years ago, glacial till was deposited throughout the peninsula, forming hilly moraines and plains. The present shape of both the Great Lakes and Michigan's peninsulas was formed about 2,500 years ago as a result of glacial ice and meltwater action and elevation changes of the lakes' outlets.The mixed organic bog soils are found in the northern two-thirds of the Lower Peninsula. There were small lakes that were created when inland lakes filled in with rich nutrients. Remains of ice mastocons and other extinct animals are sometimes found in the former bogs.

The hills and valleys, lakes and bogs create the perfect climate for growing trees of all kinds. Because of the highlands in the middle of the state and the forests, great pressure pushes the water to the low lands. There the water finds the easiest route and thus forms rivers that lead out to the shores of the Great Lakes. There are also great aquafirs that flow through the rocks underneath the visible lands that help the supply of fresh water in the state. Many rivers supply water for the horses. The AuSable River flows through the counties on the northeast side of the state and supplies the Michigan Riding and Hiking Trail with water for 2 1/2 days. The Manistee starts north of the trail and flows south allowing a good source of water in the middle of the state. The trail crosses this river and is belly deep to the average horse. Two more days riding and you find the Boardman River. The next night is the Betsy and the next day you cross over the Platte. All this water is flowing to the shores of the Great Lakes that surround the state and gives a naturalist a great feeling when he witnesses it. Somehow the flow of the water takes our imaginations with it and makes us wonder what is around the next bend, and the next. We can pretend we are the only humans on the earth.

Several species of animals are native to the regions and are often seen while riding the trail, including whitetail deer, black bear, raccoon, red fox, bobcat, woodchuck, squirrel, beaver, muskrat, rabbit, skunk, porcupine, and the reintroduced elk. Eagles, osprey, and the endangered Kirtland's warbler are less often seen; the

21

wolverine, fisher, marten, and wild bison have vanished. Several species of fish have become rare, including white fish, sturgeon, herring, muskellunge, and lake trout. Sportfish found in the state include bluegill, crappie, perch, large and smallmouth bass, pike, and salmon. Common birds include the great blue heron, kingfisher, several duck species, geese, and gulls. Many songbirds come in the summer and fill the woods with music, especially the wood thrush who sounds like a lost piccolo player throughout the day.

The summer months are warm enough to ride without a sweatshirt, with an occasional heat wave in the 90's. The rains are warm enough to ride in and not get a severe chill if you happen to get caught without a rain coat. Bugs are not great pests except in hot places protected from the wind.

Spring and Fall are great for riding and hiking if you have a warm bed for you and a good blanket for your horse.

Wintertime finds the trail covered with about 2 feet of snow but still being used by cross-country skiers and snow mobiles.

If a person thinks he is alone out there on the trail, he is mistaken. The cut-off stumps are the remains of another time when man lived in these woods. Merely a hundred years ago the woods swarmed with men called lumberjacks. They came in the winters and cut the big hardwoods and the huge white pine and dragged the huge logs to the rivers with big teams of draft horses, where they would float them down the rivers to the shoreline towns for lumber. There are thousands of miles of old logging trails that twist through the woods yet today, that are visible to a person if he knows what he is looking for. If you think about what it took to pile all that dirt up and make roads without machines it seems like an impossible endeavor, but there are miles and miles of these trails to overwhelm you. The rape of the land with all the decaying tree stumps reminds you that this was a hungry pack of men and no thought was given to reforestation. In some places the holes where whole lumber villages stood are still visible. You can pick out the cook shack, the bunk house, the store house and the barn where the horses were kept. It was another time, not long ago, that men lost their lives and so did horses, but they were too busy to mark a grave. If you stop to listen, close your eyes and pretend, you can put yourself back in those times. Listen carefully, can you hear that call of "TIMBER"? That is what this trail does for a person. Takes you back in time and makes you a pioneer.

If you are really good at pretending, you can go back even further in time and become an Indian. You can build a bark hut along the river, catch fish, hunt animals, and eat roots and berries for your food and live a good life until some white man comes along and tells you he is taking over your spot and you'll have to move along.

The time was right; the state was the perfect state to ride and camp in with a horse. The two-tracks were asking to be explored. The human race had recovered from the great depression and World War II and they wanted to play. It was a time when people wondered if they had what it took to be a pioneer and rough it. A small group of people had a big idea. Could they put it all together? They had to try.

Fitch Williams

Rex Garn, 1964

Tony Wilhelm & Fitch Williams, 1963

Sally Wilhelm, 1963

THE TEST
Ch.2

1963 was an exciting year for the small group; trails had to be connected, the media had picked up on the idea so letters had to be answered; a big fall round-up was planned for the afternoon of October 5 (Saturday) at the State Forest Campground on the Manistee River, 4 miles West and 2 miles south of Frederic, Section 7, Town 27 North, Range 4 West, Crawford County, Michigan. Groups from Gaylord, Cheboygan, Luzerne, and Traverse City were planning to ride from their respected area to convene and discuss their experiences on the trail and learn about the newly formed organization called the Michigan Trail Riders Association. Everyone was welcome.

The Grand Traverse Saddle Club would ride from the Rex Ranch, Beitner Road, Traverse City. You could keep your horse at Rex's for the night or if you didn't have a horse, you could rent one from him. If you didn't have a horse trailer, you could arrange to have it hauled by the ranch. You could also have all your gear trucked by the ranch. Food was provided by the cooks, Ernie and Evelyn Heims, from the Grand Traverse 4-H Club Camp, Gilbert Lodge, Grand Traverse 4-H Club and was guaranteed to be outstanding. Rates under today's standards were so cheap they were sickening; Breakfast - $1.75; Lunch $1.25; Dinner $2.50; Hay and Grain (per day) $1.00 and hauling gear from campsite to campsite $.50. To have horse, gear, and rider hauled back from the Round-Up; $5.00 total. Horse rental for three days including return transportation of horse: $26.00 If you couldn't make the whole ride, you could join up whenever you could make it. Reservations had to be made no later than September 28, 1963.

Fitch Williams took on the job of constructing a legal organization and making it non-profit. He had a set of county maps on his wall in his office and everytime a new section of the trail was secured, he'd mark it off with pins.

Tony enlisted the help of Fred Haskins, Head Forester for the Conservation Dept. in the Traverse City area who knew the country like the back of his hand. Tony remembers riding with Fred in a little Ford Pinto down through the two-tracks and sometimes he'd go places where Tony was sure his horse wouldn't even go. But Fred always knew the way out. The Department of Conservation was very helpful in every way.

Explorer Post 36 of the Boy Scouts put a lot of labor into the trail between Shecks and M-37. They were very instrumental in the trail that took people down the steep bank to, across Jackson Creek, and up the steep hill on the other side.

Meanwhile on the other side of the state, Jim Hardy was working with his U.S. Forest Service neighbor, Forest Rhodes, replacing two-tracks with wandering trails that led through the Federal Lands, connecting up with little lakes and crossing streams.

Western Horseman Magazine wrote about the creation of a horse trail that would go from shore to shore across the state of Michigan. Other states wrote and asked how to go about it.

One lady from Illinois who read about the trail in the Western Horseman would become very dear to the trail riders as a friend and mentor. Sally first remembers seeing Jane McGuinn for the first time at Empire in the spring of 1964, as she got out of her white Cadillac which was pulling a two-horse trailer. Everyone wondered who that old lady was. (Jane, who was in her mid fifties seemed old to the people in their early thirties.) They soon learned to love her. Sally tells us why; "Jane had a trememdous influence on the trail ride, on the organization, and on us, too. If you had a problem with your horse, she'd always come up with an answer. If you needed something, she'd dig around in her stash of goodies and come up with whatever you needed. Even on the trail, even though she used little, tiny saddle bags, she always brought out whatever was necessary for the emergency. Rex always said she even carried an anvil in there.

"She was always generous about loaning equipment out and it was contagious. Everyone was soon helping each other out and it was getting like one big family - more and more each ride. She always came with fun games for the kids to play with in camp, and the kids all loved to ride with her. She had wonderful tales to tell about her travels and experiences. Whatever age she talked to, she always used adult words, never talking down to the kids like adults often do with children. .

"Having had experiences in long distance trail riding in Pennsylvania, southern Illinois and Iowa, was something none of the rest of us had ever done. Needless to say, she soon became our mentor and we would follow her anyplace - which was not always good because she had two rules; never get off your horse and never turn around and go back. This was sometimes hazordous in the northern Michigan swamps, but follow her we did, and somehow we all survived. There was

Fred Haskins - DNR & Explorer Post 36, 1963

Jane McGuinn & VW, 1973

only one time that I can remember when Jane was a little flustered. (This story told below.) The afternoon before the last day of each ride, Jane would gather up one or two of us and head to the nearest town to pick out "trophies". These would be little dime store items to depict events, usually disasters, that had happened to people during the ride. That night at the campfire, awards would be made and everyone would have a grand time. She really is one of the greatest persons I've ever known. A marvelous person, an incredible horsewoman, we all dearly love her."

Most of the trail was quite safe for the outdoor horseman who knew how to ford rivers, test bogs and stay clear of the marl bottomed inland lakes that swallow up a horse in seconds. However, there was one mile long section that would strike fear in even the bravest of riders just east of Kalkaska. It was a swamp that looked even more scarey than the most evil of swamps Walt Disney could create. Straight through this swamp was a corduroy road (a road made of posts laying side by side to form a bottom to keep you from sinking into the muck) with the posts covered by mud so they were hidden. Horses didn't especially like to step into the mud to begin with, then when their feet would touch the round, slippery, rotting posts, they would try to go for the bogs beside the road or off into the swamp, that looked like a Florida everglade full of alligators.

Sally and Tony Wilhelm were accustomed to going through it and remember a night when they rode through it with Jane McGuinn. This black night, as they were going through late because of an accident to Sally's truck that caused Sally's arm to be in a sling, Jane was out in front as usual. All of a sudden she started to scream that she was off the trail and sinking into the bog. When Tony and Sally finally got out their flashlights and shone them on her they saw that she was caught under a tree limb that had fallen across the trail. She was on the trail and not sinking. They removed the tree limb and continued on their way. Jane was from Leland, Ill. and the mud has a bottom in Illinois. Michigan mud does not. This trail through the swamp saved 6 miles of riding the shoulder of a busy highway. It became known as Mayhem Swamp.

Fall was approaching and the group finalized their plans for the three day ride. The Traverse City group had it all worked out right to the minute. They would leave the Rex Ranch at 8:00 AM Oct. 3, 1963. Their arrival time at the Shecks Bridge would be 4:00 PM. Dinner was between 5 and 6:30. Remember these meals were catered by the cooks from the 4-H camp's Gilbert Lodge. Ernie and Evelyn Heim were known for their homemade breads, late evening snacks, family style meals.

On Oct. 4, they would eat breakfast between 7 and 8:00 AM, toss their gear into the shuttle truck and depart at 8:30 AM.via their horse. They would arrive at Log Lake,(Sec. 10, T27N, R7W, Kalkaska Co.) at 5:PM. Dinner would be served between 5 and 7:00 PM.

On Oct. 5, they would eat breatfast between 7 and 8:00 AM, again toss their gear into the shuttle truck by 8:30 AM and depart on their horse by 8:30. They were

Broegman truck & homemade trailer, 1963

Bob, Evelyn, Teri Broegman, and Jan Brackridie

to arrive at the Round-Up Grounds by 5:00 PM that evening. Dinner between 6 and 7:00 this last night. The Round-Up Grounds (Sec. 7, T27N, R4, Crawford Co.) was a people camp on the Manistee River. This was the predetermined meeting place for the three groups.

The Traverse City group accomplished their mission as planned, ate a delicious supper and had a grand party. The next day their horses were trucked back to the Rex Ranch without any problems.

The eastern group was also preparing for their trek across country to the Manistee River. Evelyn and Bob Broegman wrote to Lost Creek Sky Ranch about it and received a nice hand written letter back from the owner, Jim Hardy. It read; Sept. 20, '63, Dear Mr. and Mrs. Broegman,

Thanks for your note of Sept. 18. Enclosed is the information on our Oct. "Round Up" Ride. We would like to leave the Sky Ranch on Thursday morning at 9:00 AM. Breakfast will be served at the ranch before departure. Price includes all meals and feed for horses, served from our chuck wagon on the trail. You must furnish your own sleeping bag and personal gear, which can be transported on our chuck wagon. May I suggest an immediate reservation if you are depending on using our horses, since the number is limited. We have a very congenial group started and this promises to be a very enjoyable ride. So bring your toothbrush and a smile and join us! Sincere, Jim Hardy.

He had forgotten the prices.

Evelyn took Jim up on his invitation and her story follows:

Stories by Evelyn Broegman

Evelyn and Bob Broegman lived in Davisburg, where Bob worked as a mechanic at the Oakland County Garage. They had 6 children who all enjoyed riding and camping.

The Broegman family, including Evelyn and Bob's parents and sisters and brothers and even grandparents, had enjoyed camping together for many years. Sometimes they had ventured as far north as Guernsey Lake and Shecks before the Cross the State Trail was invented. They started hearing scuttlebutt about a group of people who were trying to make a trail to enable people to ride a horse all the way across the state of Michigan, from the shore of Lake Michigan to the shore of Lake Huron.

Two years before the first across the state trail ride they had stopped in Kalkaska to visit a barber friend named Smitty (Basil Smith). "He told us at the time that there was going to be a meeting that night at Tony and Sally's place. Then he said if we'd like to go to meet him later, we could go there together.

"So we came back and we had all our kids in the car. We left the kids to play in the car while we went in to the meeting.

"Anyway, it was the first time we had met Tony and Sally, and Rex and Jim Hardy, Fitch Williams, and Basil. They were talking about the trail and getting it going, hopefully, to get it to go all the way across the state. At this time everything

30

was just in the planning.

"After we returned home, we kept seeing articles in different papers and magazines about this trail. When I read where there was going to be a meeting place where two groups were going to converge , one coming from the west and the other from the east, I wrote to a saddle club at Empire and asked them if they were planning on going and if they might have room for us.

"They weren't sure what they were going to do, and suggested that I try Jim Hardy. So I got Jim's address and wrote to him. He wrote back and told us when they were going to leave and what they were going to do. He planned to take a pack mule and camp out under the stars. It was to be the 3rd to the 6th of October.

"When the time came to go, Bob couldn't get off work, so I started out with a neighbor, Ray Estes and his daughter Connie, my mother and my daughter Teri. We started out with a car. It was a Rambler that we could sleep in, with the horse trailer hooked on behind. I was only about a mile from home and down hill all the way, and when I got down past the lake, I tried to stop and the brakes just couldn't hold the load. So I drove on down to the county garage, which is just about a mile from our home and I told Bob that I wasn't going to be able to handle the car. So he unhooked the car and hooked up the old pickup. We realized that we had just given up our beds, but we had tarps in the back of the pickup with our hay and grain and we started on our way, north to Hardy's, for our adventure..

"On the way,there was a terrible rain storm. The truck had those vacumm window wipers and while it was pulling up the hills, the wipers would slow down so much I couldn't see and the rain was coming in the holes in the sides of the truck. I felt like I was in a washing machine. It was getting to be such a nightmare we finally stopped. Ray said he would drive my truck and I could drive his car. He had a brand new car. So we traded vehicles and continued on our way.

"We had two horses and a pony in a trailer that Bob had made and Ray had two horses. We got up to Mio and turned on M-72. We were watching for a blacktop road to the right that would take us to Jim's ranch. We discovered we had gone too far when we crossed the river. It was now about 12 o'clock at night. We managed to turn the rigs around and stopped at a house with a light on and asked the man if he knew where the Lost Creek Ranch was. He told us where it was and we headed for it. We found the road this time. There was a gas station on the corner and a sign Lost Creek Sky Ranch.We turned down it and got to Jim's. It was cold because it had been raining, so he put the horses in the barn. We didn't even bother going to the ranch house, we just crawled into the trailer and went to bed. Ray and Connie slept in their car. The ride was to start out at nine the next morning.

"In the morning we divided up our supplies into three piles for the ranch hand to bring out to the different campsites at night. We traveled with what clothes we would wear for three days (not knowing what to expect from the weather, but hoping our past experiences would serve us well) and our lunches.

"When the rest of the group rode over to where we were saddling our horses, they saw we had a pony and a small horse. They were rather upset with us because they thought we would hold them back. But our ponies were not the kind of ponies that held anybody back.

"That first day was a short day. My horse jigged most of the day and he bounced my movie camera that I had tucked into my saddle bag enough to turn it on. If we could have developed the film, we would have had a movie of what it was like to be inside a saddle bag on a jigging horse. I did take some movies while riding and they were jumpy also because of the horse's inability to take a smooth walking step! I also had taken along some eggs that I had cracked and dumped into tupperware dish. I thought if I left them for the ranch hand to bring out for his nightly trip that they might get broken. (Right?) When we got to our camping spot for the night, I discovered the eggs had been jiggled into a froth. We tried to scramble them along with some spam but they did not resemble any scrambled eggs we had ever eaten before. They didn't taste like them either. We used those little tin mess kits that fold up.

"The first day's trail took us cross country to a road that crossed the Au Sable River. We crossed on a bridge and continued on, going through an old railroad grade down through a dense cedar swamp. We came to a ditch. The group ahead all jumped their horses over it, but we, not knowing the area, decided to walk through it. Ray's horse attempted to jump it but went sideways into the swamp up to his belly in black muck. Somehow he managed to get out and although he was a mess, he was not hurt. The rest of us got off and walked the horses through, then continued on.

"Our camp that night was on the bank of a branch of the Au Sable River. I had lost my gloves just before getting into camp, and I knew I'd freeze my hands without them. Well, we made camp, built a fire in a hole where an old stump had once been, but couldn't get any heat out of the fire. We fixed our simple meal and wished we'd eaten out of cans instead of trying to cook spam and eggs. Instant soup mix and hot drinks we managed to fix and they were good. We didn't give our horses too much of their feed, planning on giving them more later, but when we went to get the rest of our hay, the other people had taken it all to put under their sleeping bags for mattresses, leaving us nothing.

"The nights come on fast in October. We had summer sleeping bags and a tarp over us for a shelter. We propped up our saddles for our heads, and laid our saddle blankets on the ground for ground cloths. It was cold. The moon came up full and it looked to be as big as the earth looming over us. We three huddled together the whole night. We looked over at Ray and Connie who had made the same preparations we had and noticed he had taken off his boots. We kept wondering how he kept from freezing his feet. All night the moon shone icy white on us and we thought the night would never end. It froze the ice on the edge of the river.

"By morning we rose and tried to get a fire going to cook our meal. Our wash cloths were frozen on the rope and our soap wouldn't pour out of the bottle, so we did the best we could to clean our camp dishes. We prepared our lunches from

Ernie & Evelyn Heim

Evelyn Broegman & Jubilee, 1968

the supplies in our tin pail brought out by the ranch hand the previous night, which had frozen also. We prepared our breakfasts over sterno cans and used a folding gas stove to cook on when we needed more heat. We felt bad that our horses had not had enough to eat. We prepared for the second day's ride.

"Our ride on this day took us into the Army practice range with a lot of deep sand for the horses to walk through. We were warned to always stay on the small trail roads because there were possibly loaded shells laying around that had not gone off yet. The trail took us to a small lake, all sandy with a hard bottom. The weather had warmed up and it made us feel good. We camped early and gave the girls some time to play. We all waded into the lake to wash our feet and faces. The ranch hand had brought us our supplies and my mother set about to make a makeshift tent. She said we were not going to sleep out in the open another night. We hung a rope between two trees and threw our tarp over it making a two-sided tent so we could all sleep together. The ranch hand had brought out our food and sleeping bags, and hay for the horses. We had a little better meal that night.

"Our group kept to ourselves, the others didn't visit very much.

"We slept warmer that night but morning found the girls not feeling well. We went on as we had no other way to go but ahead. It was our last days ride and we felt we could make it. The trail continued on through the army area going down the Lewiston Grade to where it goes under the I-75 expressway, then we rode two tracks to the high range of hills before getting to the Manistee River. There was a big steel fire tower on this ridge.

"The pack kept slipping on the pack horse today and many stops had to be made to adjust it.

"It was here on the ridge that Jim stopped to spruce everybody up and tie ribbons to the tails of some of the horses, signifying kicking horses. Jim had previously checked out a spot to cross the river beside a red cabin. The banks were steep, but the bottom was firm. As we entered the water, the river was too deep for the ponies and they had to swim. Ray and Connie changed horses mid-stream and we continued on up river to the place where the west group could see us fording the river at the campsite. When we reached the spot where we were to make our grand entrance, there weren't any people. Apparently they had moved down to the next campground.

"Upon going out of the river on the other side, (another steep bank), Mom's horse slipped and she fell off. She didn't get hurt, but the horse had got his foot caught in a root. She made it to the top of the river bank and we all went on to find the other camp. We had just arrived when the ranch hand came to take us back for our rigs. We hurriedly picketed the horses and leaving the girls with Mom, Ray and I rode back to the Lost Creek Sky Ranch looking forward to getting into some dry clothes. We tried to watch all the road signs so we could find our way back to our camp.

"It was dark by the time we got to the ranch so we started back right away.

Vera & Dawn Broegman, 1968

Connie and Ken (Ray) Estes

It was fifty miles back to camp and by the time we got there it was quite late. We found my mother leaning against a tree wrapped up in a tarp shivering from the cold. She was upset because the girls had gone down to the river to where the west group and east group were eating a wonderful supper and having a party. We were so tired, we picked up our gear and made our beds in the trailer, fixed our dinner in the warmth of it and went to bed. Finally, a good bed of straw and heat from the gas stove made our night comfortable. Our horses had a good feed of hay and grain and they were happy."

(Description of the Broegman trailer: Bob had built a trailer on a house trailer frame. He made it for 2 horses in back and the front part would hold 2 ponies. The very front of the trailer had a counter where we had a 3 burner gas stove with bottle a of gas. We had a 3 drawer cupboard which we used for cooking, storage of food and dishes, etc. We also had space for all our needs up there too. 1 window in front, a side door, 2 windows on the side for fresh air. We kept hay, grain and saddles in the truck until the '64 fall ride when we had a small camper on the truck for us and hay in the trailer. When our boys went, we put up bunk style beds over the stalls using the plywood board between ponies and stove area and we slept on the floor.)

"We had taken movies of our trip, but they were a bit topsy, being taken from the back of my jigging horse. This is the only time I got to ride my horse, Cherokee, on the Michigan Trail. My husband and Teri rode him. I had my other horse (Jubalee) broke and I rode him.

"We drove home the next day and can say it was an experience we all would never forget. Despite all the cold, rain and not so good food, the beauty of the ride was worth it all. The leaves were in full color and the days were sunny. I'm glad I was young enough to enjoy it and often wondered if I could have done it if I'd been my mother's age. Never the less, we all continued to ride together for many years."

Evelyn and Bob Broegman became fond supporters of the Michigan Trail Riders Association missing only 1 ride in 31 years. Bob has handled the job of trail boss for 17 years.

The Fall "Round-Up" ride was a great success. Plans were made for the winter projects of a guide book and the drawing up of by-laws for the new Michigan Trail Riders Association. Everyone involved was ecstatic that they had created a trail that could get a person all the way across Michigan from shore to shore. They couldn't have imagined, in all their wildest dreams, how many people would pick up the challenge over the next 30 years. Hopefully, the trail will be there forever.

THE FIRST RIDE ALL THE WAY
Ch. 3

You cannot imagine how the idea of a trail across Michigan caught on with the horse populace. People wanted to ride this trail. The small little group of friends who, in the past, could ride their horses for fun every weekend, found themselves working for the success of the now prospective trail ride across the state.

They had to establish campsites; which meant cutting brush for parking places for trucks and horse trailers; putting up picket posts for ropes for picket lines to tie horses to; help make signs and corner posts for markers; and to plant them at strategic places; help mark the trail; answer letters; and try to plan a ride for June of 1964.

They needed a place to start on the shore of Lake Michigan. When they approached Empire with the idea, the Lions club was excited about the trail starting there. They took over the job of laying it out and marking it. They generously allowed the horses and people to camp on their baseball field.

Basil Smith, the barber in Kalkaska who kept his horse in back of his shop, painted metal arrows blue and marked the trail from Guernsey Lake to Kalkaska. He also was very instrumental in getting the town to let the trail riders camp just outside of town beside the landfill. He always met them with hot coffee whenever they rode through.

They now had to form a governing agency to conduct meetings and provide supervision and direction both on the trail and in the camps. Some of the trail was not marked yet so they feared people would get lost. Also, many of the people inquiring were new to camping with a horse and needed guidance to avoid accidents. They called their organization the "Michigan Trail Riders Association".

First of all they needed a Trail Boss. This person would be responsible for the supervision of the trail ride, and would appoint members various jobs as he saw fit.

Second; they needed a Trail Guide. This person would be responsible for locating the trail and directing the people on it. He would be responsible for keeping an accurate log book and a record of the trip. This position would have to be held by a person from the Department of Conservation and another one from the National Forest Service. (The land east of I-75 is mostly Federal Forest lands, while the lands west are mostly State Forests.) This meant that either Fred Haskins or Forest Rhodes would be the men in charge of this duty.

Third; they needed a point rider who would lead for the day and set the pace. This person would also call for rest stops and be generally aware of the entire group, keeping them somewhat together. This point rider should be extra cautious when crossing ravines to prevent the lead horses from running up the opposite hill. (for you who do not understand horses, this would cause the rear horses to run down the ravines and possibly trip and fall.)

They felt there was also a need for a Flank Rider who would ride with small groups of riders within the ride, and keep them from stringing out too far. He also had to give aid where needed, assist in all road and water crossings, and when crossing ravines would prevent horses in his group from running up the opposite hill.

A Drag Rider was also needed, to keep strays and stragglers moving, close gates, and watch for articles dropped on the trail.

In camp they needed a Camp Boss to designate the locations where horses were to be picketed, and supervise the tieing up of all horses; point out where the tents and other sleeping accommodations were to be set up; send people after wood; find people to help the camp cook; wake the camp in the mornings; and generally supervise the breaking of camp so that the riders would be ready for departure at the designated time. He must also make sure all litter was properly disposed of.

Required equipment for each working member of the organizations was; a good saddle, a rope, a first aid kit, hoof pick, matches in waterproof container, jack knife, wire cutters, and a compass. One member should be assigned to carry a small hammer, snub-nosed nippers and a hoof knife for minor repairs.

They were reminded that the ride was to be a pleasurable trip for the riders and they should not be regimented. Their sole function was to provide safety, comfort and pleasure for everyone.

What an undertaking for our small group. They had no idea what kind of riding credentials their new perspective trail riders would have. Nor, what kind of horses would they expect to ride 220 miles in any kind of weather.

Fred Haskins ~ Shecks, 1963

Following the AuSable, 1964

The spring of 1964 arrived right on time and people started writing for information about the big trail ride across Michigan starting on June 20th and ending on June 28th.

Questions such as; If I am dropped off at Empire with my horse and gear, can I find a ride back to Empire when we get to the other side of the state? Is there any way I can get to Mass on Sunday morning? What kind of equipment should I bring? Can I buy my hay and grain from someone on the ride? Can I bring my dog? Will there be a veterinarian on the ride? How about a farrier? How much does it cost? Will we have to cross water? Do we ride if it rains?

They might as well have asked if Whipporwills attack after dark or do frogs bite the horses when they cross through mud puddles!

June 19, 1964, finally arrived and more than 40 people came to Empire to ride across the state of Michigan on horseback.

The first day's ride on the trail went as planned. They rode in a group cavalry style. Fitch had put a lot of thought into how they could ever make such a long ride. His plan was to ride 45 minutes and walk, leading your horse,for 15. It was close to 35 miles to the first night's campsite at Mud Lake. Upon arrival most of the riders just dismounted and laid down on the ground totally wiped out.

The next morning the group starting the second day's ride was one half the size of the previous day. They proceeded as they had the day before; ride 45 minutes and walk 15. That lasted until about 11:30 AM, when they crossed M-37, then there came a woman's voice from the group that said she's had enough of that walking baloney. From then on it was ride all the time and move 'em out. The woman who spoke up was in her mid 50's and had ridden many a trail ride. Her name was Jane McGuinn, from Illinois, and her knowledge would teach the Association many important things about trail riding and caring for horses under such circumstances.

Their destination the second night was a campsite on the Boardman River near Guernsey Lake, a distance of about 35 miles. About 7:00 PM. they rode into camp with the aromas of a banquet filling the air.

The Heims' prepared banquets for the hungry riders every night, plus breakfasts and sack lunches. They had a little plywood trailer that hauled their supplies and one side opened to make a shelf. All the food was cooked out on the open fire, except the coffee. Their homemade breads and desserts sent the riders to their beds stuffed. As I mentioned before, the baked goods were prepared at the Twin Lakes 4-H Camp.

You'd think a little authenic food like flour and water, fried in buffalo fat would have been more appropo, then again, the modern cowboy's body is used to meats, salads and desserts!

The third day they had to ride all the way to the Manistee River; a distance of nearly 40 miles. This meant crossing through the swamp, appropriately named Mayhem Swamp. Actually, at this stage of the trail, the corduroy road was not too bad, if you stayed on it. It was after the gas company put a pipe line through, that the water started finding different pathways underground and made every step a guessing game. In the warm months there were the deer flies zooming in on you and your horse by the hundreds, making your horse want to run anywhere just to escape them.

I rode through this swamp at this point in time with eight children. One little girl's horse had the idea whenever there was a culvert across a road that it was not to be stepped over. This mare thought it better to go around the end. I almost lost the kid on the east side of the state twice and when I saw that swamp, I was sure I would lose her in it. By now the little girl was getting better at preventing the bypass trick which actually saved her life. When her mare saw the culvert and made a lunge for the end of it, the girl grabbed her one rein in both hands and brought her back over it. This caused the mare to leap high in the air and she landed on the rearend of my horse. We slowed her down and she got back on the center of the road.

The trail riders were starting to tire by the end of this third day. They came up with the idea that if they thought they only had four miles to go they could make it. So they kept saying only four more miles, only four more miles. That saying still holds today. If you see a greenhorn on the trail and he makes the mistake of asking you how far to camp, you get to say, "Only four more miles!" It doesn't matter how many it really is. They even made up a song about it to the tune of "Three Blind Mice."

Rex realized his horse was getting tired, so he led it the last five miles into camp. They got in a 7:25 PM.

On the fourth day they crossed the Manistee River and headed east. This river is about belly deep to the average sized horse where they crossed. I'm sure there were a couple of the horses that needed to be pulled by a rope. That is always an exciting ride, especially if you fall off as the horse lands in the water, after leaping about eight feet into the air.

They went through the town of Frederic and on eastward near I-75 before turning south. They had to go into the city limits of Grayling to find a road that would take them under I-75. Five or six miles southeast found them at the Corwin Farm. Mr. Corwin had a field that he let the riders camp in while graciously providing water for the horses. He loved to talk to the horse people. They had only ridden about 25 miles that day which allowed them to arrive about 5:00 PM.

The fifth day was another 25 mile day from the Corwin Farm to Lost Creek Sky Ranch. This section of the trail rode through a lot of scrubby jack pines which keeps out the breezes and makes a perfect set-up for gnats. One particular part of this trail became known as Death Valley. Arrival time this evening was 4:30 PM. Sixteen people kept hanging in there. Some people came to ride just for the day and others started the ride at the Manistee River.

The Sixth day took them from the Lost Creek Sky Ranch to McKinley campground on the AuSable River near the town of McKinley. Arrival time 3:30 PM. About 25 miles.

Dedication Sign - Kalkaska Camp - 1964

Cleaning beaver dam out of culvert in Mayhem Swamp

Doc Lannen, his wife Jean, and office girl Betty Bartek, started the ride at the Corwin Farm. Doc kept a log of his experiences and if it weren't for his stories, this book would be very boring. From his memoirs; "Just as we were approaching the McKinley Camp, one of the men knocked out his pipe on his boot. Woosh! The prairie was on fire, but fortunately there were enough riders present to stomp out the fire. It was a good lesson at a good time. It taught us on the first ride to have a respect for fire and we are still warning people to make sure their fires are out before leaving them unattended."

Doc also tells about his first real meeting of the group; "My wife, Jean and our office girl, Betty Bartek, met up with the trail riders at Lost Creek Sky Ranch on Wednesday night. The next day we rode to McKinley Camp. It was a very hot, dry day and especially dry because we had but one pint of water for the three of us all day. We set up our camp on the bank of the AuSable on Consumers Power property. After dinner we decided to go to the McKinley bridge to go swimming. We hauled several in our horse trailer, but five of the riders (Tony and Sally Wilhelm, Albert and Deedee Schultz and Rex Garn) floated down the river on air mattresses. We got there ahead of them and went swimming. Soon we heard the others coming down the river. We heard the voice of Rex ask a fisherman upstream from us where they were. The latter explained that this was the McKinley Bridge. Rex exclaimed, 'Thirty five miles on this damned raft today. Hey! Where is my wife?' 'Phyllis' he hollered at the top of his lungs. Unbeknown to the fisherman, his wife Phyllis, was home in Traverse City, taking care of the ranch.

"After we had finished swimming, we were getting ready to return to camp when Rex came and asked if he could borrow ten dollars. He explained that they were going to the bar and as they had arrived in swim suits they had no money. As I had not really gotten acquainted with him, I did not know whether he could be trusted or not, but thought I could afford ten dollars to find out. He promised to pay me when they got back to camp, but as we had gone to bed when they returned, I did not see him until the next morning. We were standing in the chow line when he approached and handed me the money. I thanked him and told him that I thought that he was the kind of a guy that would pay off a bet. I do not remember what he said, but as many ears were pointed towards us, he arose to the occasion. I might mention that in later years we were to become close friends and I thought very much of him as did all who knew him."

The seventh day they left McKinley camp at 8:15 AM. This was a particularly pretty day riding along the beautiful AuSable River. Sally Wilhelm remembers Jan McGuinn finding a rattlesnake in the trail and holding it down with a stick until someone could kill it. Sally had the skin of that rattler on the cantle of her saddle for many years.

On this day they passed by the Curtisville Store where cold drinks could be purchased. (People still stop there today.) They arrived at Stewart Creek Camp at 5:30 PM. Stewart Creek is a little creek that empties into the AuSable.

On the eight day, they left Stewart Creek Camp at 8:15 and got into Gordon Creek Camp by 2:30. This was a real campground with water pump, pit toilets, and other people camping.

The ninth (last day) they left Gordon Creek Campground at 10:40, rode to Trails End Dude Ranch, and on into Tawas by 2:40 PM.

From Doc Lannen's memoirs again; "Fitch Williams was in the lead when we rode into Lake Huron at the end of the ride. Jim Hardy rode up from behind, leaped on Fitch's back and dumped him into the water. Riding into Lake Huron was a thrill for all of us but for those who had ridden all the way across the state it must have really been something special."

No doubt it was, no doubt it was. To set a goal facing unknown factors and to succeed is so rewarding there are usually never the right words to describe the feelings. I will leave it to your imaginations.

Rex Garn

44

Betty Barteck serving breakfast, 1967

Rex Garn shoeing pony, 1967

Standing left to right: Marvin Curry & Bill Hickman - horse wranglers.
First Crossing group: Harold Pence, Art Lundy, Tony Wilhelm, Rex Garn.
Sitting: Darlene Lundy, Sally Wilhelm, Jane McGuinn

Standing left to right: James Hinkle,Fitch Wiliams, Jim Hardy,
Albert Schultz. Kneeling: Mary Jo Neidlinger, Joanne Sperry,
Marilyn Blonfield, Elizabeth Williams, Jan Schultz

THE TASK OF CREATING A TRAIL RIDE
Ch.4

I envy these people who headed out to cut a pathway 240 miles long across the state of Michigan, through woods, swamps, over or through rivers, until they met the boundaries of the water's edge and could ride no further.

I envy them because the politics of that time did not inhibit them, it helped them.

In this day and age there are so few things left to conquer, most of us spend our lives watching other people via sports, science or impossible feats like mountain climbing. Some of us love to study about how our forefathers explored, captured and conquered our country. Our lives, today, do not depend on sinking an arrow into the belly of a mastodon!

Today (1995) this quest would be impossible or at least so forbidding, it would not be worth the political battle. It is very hard today, to convince the state to allow horse people the run of the woods. We do our share of tearing up the ecosystem, chewing up trees, knocking down river banks, leaving piles of rotting manure in campsites, not to mention the liability lawsuits that plague the state because it allows us to play on public lands. All this stifles any forethought of generosity. Even though most of us horse people try to save the earth, it is easy to witness carelessness and downright destructiveness as we ride the trails enjoying natures scenery. What we witness is human invasion of the forests and to keep asking the state for more land and more trails is ludicrous when we don't even take care of what we have been given.

This group that set about to make a trail all the way across Michigan in 1964 did not have to deal with the bad rapore brought on by the overuse of the land. Their endeavor was to create campsites and mark the trails leading from one to the other, a very positive goal indeed. Every weekend found them working somewhere clearing a little place in the woods or along a river for a future campsite. Designated people rode the trails and sprayed little splotches of blue about every 1/4 of a mile on the trees. Corner posts were planted at many corners with the insignia of the Riding and Hiking hoof print and human print routed into them, along with routed arrows pointing in the direction in which you were to turn. The idea was to mark the trail so that anyone could ride or hike the trail and find their way. This way the people could spread out and ride at their own pace. Also riders and hikers could use the trail anytime of the year and find their way. Nights would find them routing signs and painting posts, each 4x4 post had to be painted blue on the top with the same blue color that marked the trail. In the beginning wells, toilets, and picket posts were not used. The group little comprehended how fast their idea would spread to the horse public and how soon they would need these necessities.

By 1965 their membership had grown to 50 families. Maps had to be created showing the new trail. A guidebook was drawn up with trail and campground rules, places to find services along the way, helpful hints about camping with horses, and how to find the camps by the roads so you could get your rig into the camps.

This first book was a thin book with a spiral binding. It came with a membership to the Michigan Trail Riders Association, which could be purchased at the Wilhelm store in Traverse city, in person or through the mail. Its cost was $5.00.

A June ride was planned for 1965. It would start on Monday, June 21st at Elberta, on Lake Michigan and ride to the Corwin Farm, the campsite four or so miles southeast of Grayling, ending there June 25th. (Elberta, a town south of Empire right on the shore was a nice place to camp when the group first started the rides, however, as more people joined, it was found to be very difficult hauling a horse trailer through the deep beach sand to park for the night. It was abandoned a few years later for two reasons: 1. There was a high bluff not far from the water's edge that prohibited very many from camping there. 2. The route to Mud Lake involved a lot of road riding.) You could provide your own food or eat the delicious food prepared by the Heims off the chuck wagon. If you wanted this service it would cost you $24.50 for the five days. It's hard to believe you could eat like that only 30 years ago.

There was also a fall ride planned for 1965. It would start at Cadillac on October 13, and ride to Shecks Bridge, taking three days, and once at Shecks, they would circle ride through Sunday the 17th. They anticipated the fall colors to be at their peak around that time.

Because the rides were drawing more people, more services had to be provided; already three ranches offered horses for rent. Now the people who jumped the rigs to the next camp, needed rides back to their horses. There were too many for a car, so the big stock trucks were enlisted into the jobs. The rig drivers would follow the big stock truck to the next camp, park where he planned to camp that night, and hop into the back of the open truck for a ride back to where he left his horse tied to a post. These were fun to ride in, as a matter of fact. Sometimes they carried a dozen, and sometimes they carried 50 people. There would be hay bales to sit on and other trail paraphernalia to step over. There would always be a story teller or a joker amongst the group. Jiggling along the back roads, choking from the dust and the exhaust fumes, keeping your eyes squinted to keep out the hay chaff, keeping your ear cocked so you wouldn't miss anything, all made for an experience few would ever forget. I can still see a certain older gentleman sitting on a bale of hay, asking any of us if we knew how the rapist kept the deaf mute from telling on him. After he saw us all look at him with blank stares, he answered; "he broke her finger". He must have been waiting for months to spring that one on us. This was really where you got to know a lot of people, because once they got on their horses, they spread out over the trails and you wouldn't see many people all day. Rex's big stock truck was used for years. The people affectionately named it "Big Red".

Rex Ranch and Lost Creek Sky Ranch both offered horses for hire. They would truck them in on these big stock trucks, drop the ramp and the horses would run down to be caught by someone standing at the bottom. It was even more amazing watching them go up the ramp to go home, when some horses won't even step one step into a horse trailer. Most of the time the driver tried to unload by a bank to make the grade less steep. You could also buy hay off these trucks, or have your gear hauled from camp to camp, if you were tenting. Eventually, there had to be a fee of $1.00 a day charged for those that needed a ride.

The whole atmosphere was happy, chidling, and fun loving. For instance; One night at Goose Creek, Rex decided to take a nap in a horse trailer. His "friends" decided it would be fun to turn the trailer around so that when he opened up the back door to get out, he would step off the bank into the Manistee River. They struggled, and quietly grunted and groaned turning the front end around to line the backend up just right. When they looked inside to see if Rex was still asleep, he was holding his stomach, and trying to keep from laughing out loud.

Another little trick taught Doc Lannen how fun loving they were; "The stretch of trail between Lost Creek Sky Ranch and Smith's Bridge, across the AuSable, can be hot and miserable. We got a late start in the morning (almost noon), so by the time we arrived at the bridge we were all nearly 'punch drunk'. Nearly all rode out into the river to water their horses and to splash water on each other. As I had on some new western boots, I carefully watered my horse and then let him eat grass while I leaned over the bank to splash water on my face. Rex Garn came up from behind and gave me a push on my bottom end that was sticking up in the air and rolled me into the river. He said, 'Here Doc, this is how you clean up in a river.' I went in, new boots, billfold and all."

Doc's ability to accept their sense of humor won him many friends and he

49

later was elected president for three years and served on the board for fifteen.

From Doc Lannen's memoirs; "As long as the Rex Ranch was in operation their big red stock truck was used for transporting drivers back to the previous campsite after jumping their rigs to the new campsite each day. There might be as few as a half a dozen or as many as sixty riding in the back of "Big Red". A couple of experiences stand out in my mind...On one particular ride, after moving our rigs to the new camp and all the rig drivers had clamored onto Big Red, we found it to be quite crowded. Harvey Wild, an especially nice family man, stated that he had room on his lap for any girl under 60. Gwen Grinage quickly spoke up, 'Well, I like that.' Harvey's face turned red, 'I'm sorry, Gwen. I've got room on my lap for any girl under 70.' 'That's better,' chuckled Gwen.

"I was president of the organization the year (1968) we rode from Elk Hill to Shecks. On the last day of the ride Big Red was not especially crowded. I was stretched out flat on the floor reminiscing about the ride and I thought it had turned out quite well. I suppose I may even have dozed a little bit, but I do remember people laughing and enjoying themselves. When we arrived in camp I stood up and turned to face to the gang plank. When I went to take a step I then discovered that I had been hogtied. Someone, I think Sharon Day (Carpenter) was the guilty soul."

Rex, himself, had a little conflict with Big Red one night. Phyllis remembers it quite well; "We used to shuttle the horses we rented out to the rides back home again during the nights. I had a van with a horse trailer and Rex would drive the stock truck (Big Red). On one such night, my van ran out of gas, so Rex decided the thing to do was to siphon some gas out of Big Red's tank and transfer it to mine. He couldn't get any gas with his teeth in, so he took them out and set them on the door where you step to get into the truck. He filled the container, started back for the van and with a swing of his hand - slammed the door of the truck shut. The teeth were crushed. We continued on home. Rex had no choice but to go back because he had horses to rent out and his job of hauling people back to their horses in the mornings was of utmost importance. When he arrived back in camp it was quite obvious that he had no top teeth and he took a verbal beating. Later, during the day, people would come up to him and tell him that they also wore false teeth. One of the women who confessed lived to regret it dearly, because for years to come, at any gathering where she was, Rex would pretend that he was going to expose her and she wanted to kill him. I managed to get the teeth fixed during the day and brought them to Rex that night. He was very grateful."

This story exemplifies the fact that the trail rides that our small group had created, changed their old fun camping trips quite severely. Because of the distance from civilization, the locations of the camps made for great privacy. However, sometimes pertinent decisions had to be made by the most qualified man or men. From Doc Lannen's memoirs; "It had been a very hot day and I was administering electrolytes orally to many of the horses who looked to be in dire need. Rex started pointing out that he had these hives all over him and his throat was swelling shut. I

Riding in the back of Big Red

Big Red coming into camp, 1967

thought it sounded like an allergy to something, so I asked another doctor (Dr. George Stump, a urologist) if he had any antihistamine. The doctor did and gave some to Rex, making him chew it so it would get into his blood stream quickly. Rex was told to lay down and be quiet on a cot they borrowed from Bob Barlow.

"I went on administering my salt. Pretty soon someone called that Rex was unconscious. We decided we had better get him into Grayling, to the hospital. We used the cot as a stretcher and put Rex into the back of my suburban and took off. Dr. Pete Alferris (a pathologist) sat in the back with Rex, while Dr. Stump sat up front with me. Before we made it to the road, Pete informed us that Rex was coming around and that the trip might not be necessary. I said that I needed gasoline and film and would just as soon continue. George thought it a good idea also, and if Rex was O.K. when we got into Grayling, he would get him some cortisone. If not, we could get him into the hospital. He then said, 'Rex, I don't know if you are well enough to comprehend this or not, but you should know that you are being attended by three outstanding men in their respective fields. However, what ails you is not covered by our respective fields.'

"As parking spaces in Grayling were scarce that evening, I left both doctors at a drug store and then found a parking space at Spike's Tavern. I then went to find the doctors. When we got back to the truck, Rex was feeling much better. He said that it was a hell of a note to tell him he could not smoke or drink, and then leave him in the parking lot of a tavern. Because Rex had not eaten anything different, the men concluded that he must have been stung by a bee. Bees liked to nest along the trail in the deeper hoofprints."

Another story concerning the lack of modern conveniences is told by Pat Worden; "Sally and I were riding through the woods along the designated trail when I started feeling pain in my lower intestines. Pretty soon I was dying of pain and just had to make a nature call. I left Sally holding my horse and headed way back into the woods. I went so far back I was out of sight of Sally. Thinking I was safe, I hunkered down and was feeling some relief, when a bunch of riders started heading right for me. I then realized that the trail had wound around through the woods and was going right in front of me. I couldn't move so I just pulled my jacket up over my head, hoping no one would recognize me. Of course they knew who it was, because they had all just passed Sally back down the trail holding my horse. I learned to check out where the trail went for later nature calls."

Tony remembers a time when his son's small horse went lame midway between camps. Sally made him get off his horse and lead it, giving his horse to the boy. Tony would lead the pony along, trying to get it to stop eating, and have to trot to catch up. Then he realized that it wasn't limping. He got on the strongly built little thing and with his feet hitting the stumps as they trotted along, caught up with the group and said, "There's nothing wrong with this pony, I want my horse back."

52

Gwen Grinager

Big Red ~ Phyllis Garn , 1966

Breakfast on the trail, 1966

Ernie Heim serving Dick (Doc) Lannen ~ Clara Knunzel

Dr. Stump

Sally Wilhelm - AuSable River - McKinley Camp

Pat Worden - Trail Boss

Tony Wilhelm, 1963

Doc Lannen & Jinx and Jean Lannen & Lynx

Fitch Williams

Playing in the Manistee

THE DEMANDS OF SUCCESS
Ch. 5

In 1966 the trail riding group decided to call a meeting of all the members. They called it an annual meeting. They set up a board of directors and officially elected officers. They also set up some basic by-laws and talked about the future of the trail.

The need for water for human drinking and sanitary facilities became apparent. In the beginning old outhouses were scavaged from other campgrounds that were getting new ones. The holes had to be dug by hand labor by the members. Anyone who could get their hands on a truck that could haul a small building was appointed the job of fetching it. They were the single hole type with a pail looking stand with a metal seat with a cover you were supposed to always keep down. (I never could see the purpose because it wasn't a tight fit, quite the opposite, and there were always flies and bees buzzing in the pits. Not exactly the quiet, reading room we were used to at home.)

I remember one morning, at the old Kalkaska camp, I entered the womens outhouse and found a terrible mess. It was on the seat, behind the seat, on the floor, and on the wall behind the seat. I simply backed out and went over to the other outhouse. After all, an outhouse is an outhouse. I grew up with them. I locked the door and went about my business. The line formed outside and was strictly of the male gender. When I opened the door, to their surprise, I was a woman. The second one in line said, "I thought this was the men's." As I stepped out and walked away,

I said, "Well it isn't, it's the women's."

They stood there looking at each other for the right answer. A while after that they started putting the gender over the doorway.

Wells had to be driven, some by hand. They were made to work with hand pumps. These were paid for by the membership money. Some of them were so deep it took more pumps on the handle to get the water to the top than to fill the pail. But the water was always cold and refreshing after a long, hot day in the saddle.

Another big job was the setting of picket posts. These posts were often old telephone or light company castoffs which required someone with an inside track to get them delivered to the campsites. Then, at a work bee people would come with post hole diggers and set the posts in a row so many feet apart allowing a rope to be hung between two of them, to tie lead ropes to, securing horses for the night in a safe manner. Picket Posts were important because they kept the horses from being tied to trees which they chose to destroy - at least one nightly. This destruction of the trees, either by debarking or pawing and exposing the root systems, would soon become a thorn in the government's side as they witnessed what was happening to the woods they had in their stewardship. This in turn would cause our trail riding group many headaches trying to educate both horse and human.

1966 would be the second offering of a trail ride that would ride from shore to shore, starting at Gordon Creek on the east and riding to Elberta on the west. Horses could be trailered to Tawas the day before the ride and ridden out to Gordon Creek to make the official shore to shore trek. It was a great success, BUT; Inexperience was showing up everywhere; People did not bring along the right rain gear and would end up cold and crabby by the end of the day; horses were getting tangled up in their lead lines when tied to the picket lines because the ropes were left too long; the signs of poor fitting tack showed up in the form of girth sores and pressure bumps on the backs; people would end up with blisters on their legs and posteriors; horses would get sick because of dehydration; trucks would have engine problems and trailers would come off hitches or have flat tires; horses would lose shoes; people would get lost; the list could go on for two more pages.

Two different situations that were witnessed by many occured because of the friction of human bottoms and saddles. The first was seen because the two men in the tent who thought they were descretely applying salve to each others blisters were unaware that a bright light in a tent allows everything going on in a tent to be seen outside in sillouettes. The second was at Smith Bridge when a man wearing white levi's dismounted and unknowingly displayed two big red blood stains on the seat of his pants. He was a clothing salesman and had come dressed to the hilt.

People would get a bit ouchy after a day in the saddle riding through the wilderness. For instance, one particular day Sally Wilhelm and Pat Worden remember very well went like this; Sally started the morning going about her motherly duties of getting the two children and Tony fed their breakfasts, packed their lunches, gathered the necessary clothing for the day, made sure the dog and cat

Mary McIntyre & Marse Radtke

Digging Latrines

were in the camper to go with the rig, gathered all the tack the four horses would need for the day, saddled the horses while Tony jumped the rig, tied on the clothes, tucked in the lunches, rode all day with the family and friends, answered a million questions from new trail riders, got into camp a wee bit tired, took care of the horses, and took to her camper for a relaxing drink and some peace and solitude. Just as she was getting the first taste of the delicious fluid there came a knock on her door. It was Pat Worden, who was the trail boss that summer and she had some other people with her. Pat said, "These people saw your dog steal a loaf of bread off their table." That was the final straw for Sally that day. She opened her cupboard and found her one remaining loaf of bread and threw it at Pat yelling, "It wasn't my dog, here, give this to em." The woman walked off with the bread and Sally slammed the door of the camper. She wasn't happy again until after cocktail hour.

Another stolen food incident was when Phyllis Garn had brought over a whole meal to the old Kalkaska Camp. She had spent the whole day frying chicken, and preparing potatoes and vegetables. She spread them all out on the picnic table, turned her back for a second, and when she turned around, every piece of the chicken was gone. She knew the dog that took it and was really mad, but she decided not to raise a fuss.

The wrong horses were known to get loose in the night. There was a couple who were astute members of the organization; Dr. Stump (the same urologist that treated Rex's bee sting) and his wife, Alita. Dr. Stump rode a stallion and his wife rode a mare. The wife thought her husband's stallion to be ugly. One night they heard noises outside their trailer and in looking found the stallion breeding the mare. The mare was loose and it was her choosing. Alita sat up the rest of the night and cried because her poor mare was going to have that ugly horse's baby. George Stump didn't know what all the fuss was about because he planned to breed the mare the next spring anyway.

One other time there was a great rukus in the dark. Thinking it was George Stump's stallion again, they all rushed out of their sleeping bags to capture the cuss. When the flashlights found the guilty culprit, it was Tony's 10 year old gelding who had been castrated at a late age, breeding one of the mares. At least no tears had to be shed this time.

Doc Lannen remembers the time he got dumped in a creek and hurt his thumb. He asked the opinion of Dr. Stump. "Yes," said George, "I think it is broken. You can go to the hospital and have it x-rayed and set and it will take 6 months to heal or you can ignore it and it will take 6 months to heal." Doc chose to ignore it and he's had a crooked thumb ever since. He complained to his wife once and she said, "That's what you get for going to a urologist for a broken bone."

Doc also remembers how he learned a lesson about balls; He had a DeSoto that he pulled his trailers with, and one time when he and Jean decided to trailer out and ride there was a little depression in the road about four miles from home. The blacktop had settled and and when the back wheels of the car hit that low spot, the

Bill Zettle on a work bee

"Wild" Bill Zettle

car ducked out from under the hitch. "I told Jean that we were in trouble. However, the crossed chains held and we coasted to a stop. I got out, unhooked the safety chains, turned around and went home. I knew why it had happened. Our boat trailer took a smaller ball than the horse trailer. I had forgotten to change balls. I put the right one on, went back to the horse trailer, hooked it on and continued on our trip. That was just fool's luck."

There was another incident of the wrong ball just outside Shecks camp. The trailer had come off and went over the embankment. There was one mare in it pressed up against the manger. It took 4 men with ropes to pull her up and out of the trailer backwards. Her leg was cut quite badly and required a vet. People learned that a measly little 1/4 inch in a size of ball meant a great deal.

Enough stories for now, back to the creation of the trail.

New camps were needed because of the increase of the size of the trail rides. In 1967 the state gave them some land across from the Corwin farm. It was full of jack pine and blue berry bushes and required a lot of manpower to get in shape. The Conservation Department supplied all the materials. They needed people to install guard rails, hitching posts, stain posts, paint toilets, rake and clean up campsites, paint tables and install a few grills. The Conservation Department acted as foremen and operated the big equipment. The name of the new camp would be Four Mile Camp.

In 1968 Harold Pence passed away. He was one of the 16 who rode all the way across in 1964. He was a great advocate of the trail and helped in every way he could.

Harold Pence & Blondie

64

THE NORTH SPUR 1968
CH. 6

    The State of Michigan kindly set aside land, for a riding and hiking trail, from the Straits of Mackinaw, due south, to the town of Cadillac. At a meeting in the winter of 1968, our group of trail riders heard about this trail and decided to ride it for their annual June ride. They would ride from Cheboygan to Frederick where they would meet the main trail, ride west through Kalkaska to Shecks, and then ride south through the Hopkins Creek camp to Cadillac. There was a great deal of enthusiasm for using this section of the trail.

    Doc Lannen's memoirs; "At that time I was president of the organization. Immediately after the annual meeting in April, I received a phone call from member Norm Schmidt of Cheboygan. Norm asked if it was true that we were planning on riding down from the north. When I answered in the affirmative, he said that I had better come up and look around. He said that there were no camps except Elk Hill and that the trail was not marked, and that the end of the trail was just that: no campsite, no water and no sanitary facilities.

    "At that time I was practicing Veterinary Medicine in the Elsie - Ovid area about 30 miles northeast of Lansing. It was about 150 miles from any part of the trail and a lot farther from Merchant road.

    "I called Harold Babbitt, a board member from Frederick, and Harold and his wife, Edna, and Jean and I went up to investigate. What Norm had said was true, there was no staging area on Merchant Road, no water and no sanitary facilities, nor was the trail yet marked. This was supposed to be the start of the trail. It seemed an incredible job to have a ride in this area in only a couple of months.

"We went on into Indian River to the D.N.R. office and were given a map and told where we could set up a temporary camp one day's ride south of the north end of the trail. They said we could have a campsite anywhere on Walker Road. Just an open place in the woods.

"Bob Broegman and his wife, Evelyn, and Jean and I took two horses up for a weekend to pick a campsite. We went up on a Friday after work, pulled off the road and picketed our horses. The night was real black. Bob's horse took off into the woods and we couldn't catch him. When Bob bought the horse he was told he could never catch the horse in a pasture, he would have to be lassoed. Bob said, 'To hell with him, he can go and I don't care if he ever comes back.' We then proceeded to go to bed. Evelyn worried all night about the horse. When we woke up in the morning we heard a racket outside. There was the horse hammering on the tailgate for his grain. Bob caught him easily and fed him his breakfast.

"After everyone had eaten, Bob and I rode out to locate a campsite. I was riding Jinx, a three year old colt that later became an excellent trail horse, however, this was early in the spring and he had not been ridden that much. I pulled my paper map out of my pocket and the sound of the rattling paper sent him bolting off through the brush. A low limb caught me and brushed me off. I was hanging onto the reins, being dragged through the bushes on my back, when it dawned on me that I was not slowing him down very much. I let go and Bob took after him in hot pursuit. He found him back at the picket line about a mile from where I lost him. Jean caught him and handed the reins back to Bob. Bob found me sitting under a tree studying the map. I folded up the map, put it in my pocket and mounted my horse.

"With a workbee, we set up a temporary ' john', dug a well and marked the trail. Our well, however, was 30 feet deep, and we could not pump the water up with a pitcher pump. We had to, therefore, make arrangements to get water from a resident of the area. We also had to make arrangements with the AuSable Lodge on Otsego Lake to camp one night on their premises.

"We marked part of the trail that weekend also, but Harold Babbitt, who had a riding stable just northeast of Frederick, did the biggest share of marking that trail.

"I figured out later that I had driven more than 1200 miles preparing for this ride."

The Harold Babbitt, Doc called on for help, was by this time, a well established member of the group. He is the kind of person who keeps things to himself, but when he does speak people usually listen because whatever he is going to say has been well thought out. He and his wife Edna, have a small ranch northwest of the town of Frederick. It eventually became a camp for people riding the north spur. No matter when you needed a place to camp or water for your horse, you could always find it at Babbitt's. Harold wrote me a little note he thought might be of interest. "I personally marked the north trail spur from Frederick to the Otsego County line. I tried to get the Gaylord and Cheboygan Saddle Clubs to mark the rest of the trail to Cheboygan, but they weren't interested. Later the D.N.R. put the trail as far as Indian River. The trail used to go through the AuSable Lodge property and we used to camp there. (It is now called Michaywe). Later me and Les Botimer got permission from the D.N.R. to reroute the trail, missing the AuSable Lodge altogether.

"When my son Darryl was 5 years old he rode from Indian River to Cadillac. Jerry Chepeta was there. He took pictures of Darryl on his horse for his show. One other time, my son Darryl, my son Raymond, my daughter Vicki, my niece Susan and I were riding from McKinley. We were supposed to stop at Don Abbotts to camp that night but we missed the marker and rode all the way to Gordon Creek Camp. (The one the Hippy's took over.) It took us 11 hours."

A hundred and twenty-five riders made the 1968 June Ride from Walker Road to Cadillac. The most to date. The stretch from Elk Hill to the AuSable Lodge was 36 miles. Too far, especially in the rain. Later trail rides would stay at Harold Babbitts Ranch on Peterson Road. We were always welcomed there.

I copied Doc's memoirs like he had them written, but to anyone who does not know what the northeast part of the state is like, I want to draw a clearer picture of what our group had to endure to create this portion of the trail.

There are two roads that enter this area from I-75; One is Sturgeon Valley Road that can be picked up at the Vanderbilt exit; the other is Webb Road which is the road you are on when you turn off at the Wolverine exit. Both of these roads run east and west. They run into the one main road that goes north and south named Osmun Road. There are gravel roads and two tracks that run off from these roads like a maze, winding around the rivers on the high country. Very few are marked, so the ability to travel by compass can come in very handy.

This part of the state is made of a lot of limestone. It was also carved into moraines and kettles by the glaciers. There are patches of hardwoods, then a swampy area where the ground water comes up to the surface. This can be found anywhere, at any altitude. There are three main rivers that flow north through this region from Gaylord toward the Straits of Mackinaw. They all start east of Gaylord. The Sturgeon is the first you come to when you leave I-75. It flows into Burt Lake. The Pigeon is the second one and it flows into Mullett Lake. The third is the Black and it flows into Black Lake, just south of Cheboygan. There are two main rivers that start within ten miles of each other on the other side of I-75, on the same Latitude. The AuSable starts at Bradford Lake and flows south through Grayling, and then east to Lake Huron. Just 10 miles further west, at Lost Lake by DeWard and a swamp starts the mighty Manistee. It flows south and then west, entering Lake Michigan at the town of Manistee. There is a ridge that runs north and south in Michigan and it is quite evident when you start studying rivers. All the rivers east of this divide run to Lake Huron and all that start on the west side flow into Lake Michigan. Finding

Babbitt Ranch ~ Frederick

Judy Schlink & the gelding she lost to Swamp Fever

a trail that can be ridden by horseback and hiked on foot is tricky with this maze of waterways twisting and turning wherever it can find a path to the lakes. There are many wet areas right beside dry areas. If you see a big puddle in the middle of a two-track in the hardwoods, it could be one of those places where the limestone has cracked and the sand has drained through into the crevice and the water has seeped up into the depression. These can be far too deep for a horse to get through safely.

Because of all the water, the humidity is high and foliage grows very well. The Pigeon River Country has an interesting history. It was logged between 1860 and 1910. During the period of the 1930's, the area suffered disastrous, uncontrolled forest fires. Subsequent attempts to convert the land to farms resulted in large parts of the Pigeon River Country returning to State ownership through tax reversion and purchases.

In 1919, the tax reverted lands were designated as a state forest. Tree planting began soon after. The Headquarters was built by the Civilian Conservation Corp (CCC) in 1934-1935. In 1985, the main office building burned and has been rebuilt with the help of the Michigan Civilian Conservation Corps and donated funds from many individuals, groups and companies.

The Pigeon River Country State Forest is home to a wide vaiety of wildlife species found throughout the Lower Peninsula. Some of these species are rare in the LP such as elk, bear, bobcat, and bald eagles. In 1985, the pine marten was reintroduced. They are doing well. To provide habitat for this diversity of species, the forest is managed for a variety of tree species. It also provides many opportunities for forest recreation. It includes seven campgrounds; 60 miles of pathways; 27 miles of horse trails; several special scenic attractions; fishing on the three rivers as well as on many lakes and smaller streams; and hunting for a variety of species.

In 1918, seven elk were released near Wolverine. By 1927 they had multiplied to as many as 500. The elk herd now numbers about 1,000 animals. Limited elk hunts have been held annually since 1984. Continuing hunts are planned to achieve a balance between elk numbers, their environment, agricultural damage, and recreational viewing.

On November 1, 1990, the Director of the Department of Natural Resources signed an Order implementing the vehicle access plan, making it illegal to operate licensed vehicles on any roads not designated as open. A previous Director's Order made it illegal to operate unlicensed wheeled motorized vehicles anywhere on State land in the PRCSF. These actions were taken to help achieve several objectives from the 'concept of Management', especially 'to protect the area from over-use and over-development which would destroy its wild character.' Yet the PRCSF remains very accessible to vehicles.

Other stories from Doc Lannen's memoirs about this area you might enjoy.

"A group of us were circle riding out of Babbitt's Ranch and we had ridden over the overpass at the Waters exit on the expressway. There just happened to be a

Harold Babbitt & daughter Michelle

Daryl Babbitt, age 4, 1967

Stuckey's candy factory there that seemed like a good place to ride to. I bought a Pecan bar and put it in my saddlebag. At that time Jinx was three and still not fond of rattling papers. Betty Bartek and I were riding together when we decided to eat the Pecan bar. The trail at that point was well established and heavily wooded. When I started to unwrap the candy, Jinx heard the rustling of the papers and became spooked. I assume I swore at him and jerked on the reins. The leather strap on one end of the curb chain broke and we were off to the races. I tried to put the candy away, but the sound of the paper made him worse, so I tossed the candy up into the air and grabbed the saddle horn. I guess we would have been going yet if three teenage girls had not had the trail blocked unintentionally. Bob and Evelyn Broegman came riding up and Evelyn had some extra rawhide with which I repaired my curbstrap. Shortly thereafter Betty came riding up and said, 'Look what I found in the trail, a candy bar.' Smartass!

"On that same trail ride Betty and Cindy Smith of Ubly found some apples in an old orchard. Knowing that there was an oven in the stove in our camper, they decided to make an apple pie. It was raining hard that evening so I had put papers on the floor to soak up some of the mud. When the pie was about done the stove ran out of gas. I went out into the rain to change tanks and Sharon Day came over to see how the pie was coming. Someone (probably me) had put the shelf in the oven bottom side up so the stop did not work. When Sharon pulled the shelf out to check the pie, I could hear the word sh— clear out where I was. When I went back into the camper, here were the girls lying on their bellies, eating apple pie off the floor. The pie had turned completely over and only the upper crust was dirty.

"On one ride over to Harold Babbitt's Ranch, when I went back to get my rig I immediately got stuck in the sand. The Rex Ranch stock truck (Big Red) was there with a key in it. Bob Broegman helped me and we pulled my rig out with Big Red. On my way over to Babbitt's I met Rex riding his horse down the road. I stopped, offered him a drink from a bottle and thanked him for pulling me out. He took a drink, told me I was entirely welcome and as an afterthought said, 'but I don't remember pulling you out.

"On one of our trips to Wolverine, we had a nice weekend camping and riding and were headed for home. Norval and Hazel Ballentine had a stock truck with two riding horses and two Holstein heifers on board. The heifers had been pastured at our friend Clyde's farm all summer. Norval had to stop in Gaylord for gasoline. We were driving a 1957 Desoto and were hauling a conventional horse trailer. We did not have to purchase gasoline so we parked on the street with the motor running listening to the Detroit Tigers Ball Game on the radio. When the truck left the gas station I put our car in gear and stepped on the accelerator. The motor died and no way could I get it started again. Norval did not notice that we were not following until he was ready to pull on to the expressway. He returned and hooked on to us with a tow chain. As we had an automatic transmission it was necessary to haul us extremely fast to get our motor started. We barely made it

Sign for Elk Hill Camp

Inspiration Point ~ Rhoda Ritter & Sarah Blakeslee

72

before turning on to the ramp.

"Now that our troubles were over, we cruised right along down I-75. Suddenly Norval's right turn signal came on. He pulled off the road with me right behind. "What's up?" I queried. He said that Dodge trucks never throw rods, but that this one had done just that. They got into our car and we talked things over deciding on a course of action. We would go to the Waters exit and call their son, Rex. He would borrow a stock truck and come after us. I stepped on the starter and once again our car would not start. "What are we going to do know?" Norval asked. "I don't know about the rest of you, but I am going out into the brush and —." I answered. When I got back to the car with my nerves settled, Norval asked if he hadn't seen a can of gasoline in the trunk. He poured gasoline directly into the carburetor and the car started without hesitation. As it was then getting late, we decided that Norval had better stay with the truck, so Hazel, Jean and I went on to Waters.

"Hazel talked to Rex back in Elsie. He said he would see what he could arrange and call us back. We waited and waited and waited. Finally, Hazel called him back and he said that he had not been able to locate a truck. She told him to forget about it and that we would work something else out. I unhooked the horse trailer with the horses still in it and we went back to Gaylord and got on the expressway. We then came back to where Norval was waiting in the truck. This time we hooked the DeSoto on to the truck and hauled that to Waters. At least we were all out of the Sunday night traffic. Norval called his friend, Blackie, in Wolverine. Blackie owned the stockyards in Gaylord. He gave Norval the number of his son-in-law who owned a big truck. The son-in-law had gone to bed early as he was to take a load of cattle to Detroit Monday morning. However, he consented to come and help us out. In due time he arrived and backed his truck up to Norval's. The horses and heifers were transferred and he took them to the stockyards in Gaylord where there were many empty pens. We hooked back onto our trailer and the four of us made it home about 1:00 A.M. without further incident. On Monday we got a new fuel pump on our car and a couple of days later Norval and Rex retrieved their truck and livestock."

I threw in this story because I want you to realize how far these people from the cities hauled their horses to be able to ride in the beautiful wilderness of the north country. If and when they had breakdowns, it was usually Sunday evenings and if you did not have a local friend you could call, asking someone 150 miles away to come to your rescue was the only thing to do. I'm sure Doc Lannen and his friends were not alone with breakdowns. We have had our share of flat tires and welds coming loose on trailers coming out of the Pigeon River State Forest.

Walker Road Camp, 1968

Stuckey's Candy Factory - Waters

FURTHER DEVELOPEMENTS
Ch. 7

By Spring of 1969 there were 343 members. By Winter of the same year 69 more had joined.

Doc Lannen was looking forward to a good summer on his colt he had raised from a baby; he was getting used to paper rattling on his back. It was early morning and the plan was to cross the Manistee River to go east. The group went ahead of him into the river wherupon Doc's horse stopped abruptly when his front feet touched the water. This caught Doc off guard and he tipped forward over the horse's neck and fell head first into the river, taking his saddle with him. One of the guys (Andy Yeips) called out, "Are you all right Doc?" Doc said, "yeh." "That's good," Andy called back, "then I don't need to get all wet to help ya." At that they all rode off and left Doc standing there with his horse in the river watching his saddle blanket float away downstream. Doc had to swim down the river to get his blanket, take his horse back to the camper and change his clothes and his horse's wet blankets, and then go way around by 612 to cross the river and try to catch up with the group. Everytime he came to a hill the horse acted tired, so Doc would get off and climb the hill afoot dragging the horse up behind him. It took him until noon before he caught up. Doc knew that these people were not impressed by his clothes or the fact that he was a vet; he would just have to learn to ride better if he wanted to become a trail rider.

Even good riders lost things; Rex lost more than $500.00 cash out in the

Pat & Jim Hayes - Manistee River

Stewart Creek Camp on AuSable, 1966

Dr. Stump, Oct. 1966

The art of stump mounting

hills somewhere near Goose Creek. A small group had gone for a circle ride and found a clearing that looked like a nice place to let the horses eat grass and for the people to soak up some sunshine. When they got back to camp, Rex realized he had lost his billfold. All the money from renting horses and hauling horses and people had been in that billfold. They tried to find the clearing for many years, but either never found the right one or someone else found the billfold.

Speaking of the missing; Jane McGuinn, from Illinois, who had been coming up for every ride the group had put on since she had ridden it in 1964, was inadvertantly the cause for the saying, "Have you seen Jane today?" She loved to explore and most people couldn't keep up with her, so she would go off by herself, with her compass and maps, and her wire cutters. People would ask each other, in passing, if they had seen Jane? Many times she would be found already in camp, horse taken care of for the night, reading a book.

Reality would surface in 1970. It was in the spring that Roger Rasmussen, Regional Forest Supervisor for the Department of Natural Resources, (the same Roger Rasmussen who helped put in the well and toilets at Goose Creek,) was working on the river crossing on the Manistee River and paid a visit to the campsite he had helped create. He was dismayed at the amount of damage to the trunks of the trees and particularly, the soil compaction and root exposure caused by the horses. If this were to continue, in a few years, this grove of trees would be dead.

He had to ask the people not to take their horses in there anymore. The open area east of the river was appropriated all the way to the Manistee River Road. This seemed ample room for the growth of the organization.

Besides the damage to the camping area itself, complaints were being sent to the DNR about people riding their horses up and down the Manistee River, causing considerable turbitidy and siltation downstream. Crossing the river from one side to the other would still be allowed, but riding up and down was not in the best interest of good water management.

Our little group now had to come face to face with the fact that too many horses can ruin a good thing. They were asked to help educate other riders of this destruction to nature.

The good news of 1970 was a law passed prohibiting self-propelled motor or mechanically driven vehicles on the established and signed Riding-Hiking Trail on land under the jurisdiction of the Department of Natural Resources from the months of April, through November, in Leelanau, Benzie, Grand Traverse, Kalkaska, Crawford, Missaukee, Wexford, Otsego, and Cheboygan counties.

Stewart Creek, on the AuSable, was now too small for the number of people riding the rides so a bigger camping spot had to be found.

Doc Lannen, president that year, writes in his memiors; " For several meetings the old Thompson Farm near Rollways Campground had been discussed as a trail camp. Rex contacted the USFS but they had no money for campsite development.

"A small group put up an outhouse at the new McKinley Camp.

"Lannen wrote to Senator Hart about the high cost of putting in approved 'johns'. He also just happened to mention the fact that the organization had grown, and that bigger and better campsites were needed. Hart "nudged" the Forest Service, who responded by giving them the old Thompson Farm for a camp. They were also promised a forestland campsite to replace the McKinley Camp, which was on Consumers Land and a campsite area across from the Lost Creek Sky Ranch.

"Bud" Weaver, owner of a camper building company, announced he would build a chuck wagon for the group to use as long as they wanted. It should be ready by the fall ride of 1970.

"A workbee at the Thompson Farm was held in April of 1970. Workers cleaned up brush and cleaned the wire from an old fence row. They named it South Branch camp since it was located near the South Branch River. The Forest Service later announced they would install a pump and two outhouses at the new campsite.

"The McKinley Camp was also moved that same weekend. Some land about 4 miles west of the old camp and up on a hill was to be the new site." Doc fails to mention in his memiors that this new camp was amongst rows and rows of red and jack pine that had to be cleared.

Sally Wilhelm remembers the first time they used it; "We were all sleeping out on the ground on blankets. When I awoke, I couldn't find my collie dog. She never would get out of our sight, so I was quite alarmed. I saw the kids awake and I asked if they had seen her. They said they had gone for a ride earlier that morning and she had been with them. I saddled up my horse and headed down the trail where the kids said they had gone. When I got back to the old McKinley Camp, there was my dog, waiting in the only familiar place she could remember." Needless to say that was a happy reunion.

1970 was a sad year for the group also. On the second day of the June ride Ernie Heims suffered a heart attack and was rushed to the hospital. He recovered and went home, but later died. Jim Hardy's plane crashed while on smoke patrol and he was killed. Two key people gone would leave a big void. Without Ernie, Evelyn couldn't handle the job alone. Without Jim, they would lose a trail guide, outfitter, spokesperson with the Forest Service, and eventually the camp. Many times he helped them find their way. When he wasn't riding with them on his horse, he would keep watch for them from his plane. Once he found them riding up and down the river bank outside of McKinley, trying to find where the spot was to cross. He flew down with his plane and went across the river several times trying to tell them the right spot. Another time they were following the blue marks of a cutting and he got them back on the right trail. His ranch also catered for some of the rides, which I understand was not that great compared to the feasts the Heims's would put on.

By the fall of 1970 the Chuck Wagon was finished and a beauty it was; silver and blue, over twenty feet long, and looked like a travel trailer that you see being pulled behind cars going on vacations. Inside, it was made for putting out the meals. There were two big gas refrigerators with freezers on top, two gas ranges with ovens, double sinks with 80 gallons of water storage, hot water heater, awning for the full length of the trailer where Leona did most of her food preparation so she could visit with the people. Leona loved horses, especially palaminos. The first cook to use the new Chuck Wagon was Joe Williams. Tony St. Cyr was the second and he prepared very special meals like trout almondine, and other such delicacies. He had a Hawaiin meal at Shecks and everyone tried to creat grass skirts for the occasion.

The Fall ride in 1970 went from South Branch Camp to Harold Babbitt's Ranch, northeast of Frederick, on the trail to Elk Hill. Harold was always very gracious about letting the riders use his hay field for a campsite and would run a hose out of his barn for horse water.

By the spring of 1971 there were some changes that had to be made. Goose Creek had to be moved back from the river's edge. A new camp had to be built across the road from Jim Hardy's ranch. This new camp was on Federal Land because the Lost Creek Sky Ranch had been sold. They named it Hardy Camp in memory of Jim Hardy. Also a new well was put in at the new McKinley Camp. This was paid for by the Forest Service. They also learned that a school was going to be built on the Cadillac campground.

In the winter of '71 they decided to spend their money on a well for the Hardy Camp.

In 1972 Don Abbott volunteered to build the 'johns' for the McKinley Camp. The Forest Service would help finance them.

On the June ride of 1973 there were over 200 horses daily with 79 people riding from shore to shore. It was also decided in 1973, that the new Hopkins Creek Camp would be up on higher ground back from the creek. Vaults were set for the 'johns' and the well was shallower than expected. Elberta Camp was closed. Plans were made for the June ride to go across the state from shore to shore and back again. It was called "the double cross".

The June ride of 1974 was a great success. It went from Empire to Tawas and back to Empire. Tony Cyr catered this ride. Sharon Day was the trail boss.

Gordon Creek had to be permanently closed. The Hippy's had moved into this campground and set up house keeping. Furniture was everywhere. They eventually created so many problems the Forest Service closed the campground to everyone. They dug holes and buried the bathrooms and made big furrows around the place. Trails End Dude Ranch was offered for the trail rider's use. It was just a little ways from Gordon Creek so it worked very well.

Joe and Leona Reicha started cooking for the fall ride in 1974. They cooked for many, many years and spoiled the trail riders like the Heims' before them.

Major work had to be done to Mayhem Swamp that summer. Many bridges had to be built since the Gas Company had put a pipeline through and disturbed the flow of the water. Hardy Camp also had to have brush cleared for more campsites. A new camp at Kalkaska had to be cleared and built for the June ride. It was located northwest of town accessed by going down BeeBee Road.

The June ride for 1975 was another "double cross" with Rex Garn as the trail boss.

Near Grawn, the trail crossing a wet area near Ellis Lake, was found to be on private property and the owner had fenced it off, putting riders into a dangerous, mucky area. It looked hopeless - but Glenn Stafford offered to haul in giant telephone poles and Rex was appointed supervisor over the building of the 45 foot long boardwalk.

Local property owners near Goose Creek were feeling the crunch of the expanding camp and the increased usage of the area. A fence was put across the public road at the end of the camp and others were trying to close the camp altogether.

Meanwhile, vandals had destroyed the pump at McKinley Camp twice and caused problems at several others. Picket posts were burned.

Problems caused by the people moving out of the cities to the north created a population explosion in the north. Roads which were back country were now subdivisions. Small towns were now full of traffic making it dangerous to ride through with horses. Two-track roads became busy with cars and motorcycles. ORVs began making single trails into two tracks. The erosion caused by motorcycles made the trails deep with sand and difficult for horses and hikers. Horses were freightened by the motorcycles and accident reports flooded the roster.

It kept the Board very busy clearing up these difficulties. It meant constant communication with the government agencies, both state and federal. The Forest Service started contemplating closing the trail from Gordon Creek to Tawas. The idea of going on northeast into Oscoda was being considered.

Early in 1976, the main foundation of the whole organization was lost forever. Rex Garn passed away January 29, 1976 of a heart attack. Many mourned the loss of Rex. He was the instigator of many of the devilish things that went on amongst the group, but he was always ready to help. If anything broke down or a horse needed help, Rex would attempt to fix it. He seemed to have the inborn ability to analyse a problem and then be able to solve it. One of the Reicha boys said it best; "The rides were never the same after Rex died."

Fred Stackable made this tribute to Rex; "Those of us who had the privilege of knowing him well, knew him as a beautiful man. The better you got to know him, the more beautiful he became. He was a special man with a special heart that led him to spend untold hours on our trail so that we could enjoy the fruits of his dreams. I am sure that all of you who knew him will join me in paying tribute. Because such a man once existed, our lives and the lives that come after us have been enriched."

Enjoying the cool river

Leaving McKinley

Gordon Creek Camp

Erosion at Guernsey Lake, 1968

1974 - 1st Double Crossers - back row L to R:
Faith Aseltine, Jane McGuinn, Fred Stackable
Front row: Pat Shamber, Sandy Sperry, Jan Aseltine

Bob Barlow

1976 ONWARD HO THE WAGONS
Ch. 8

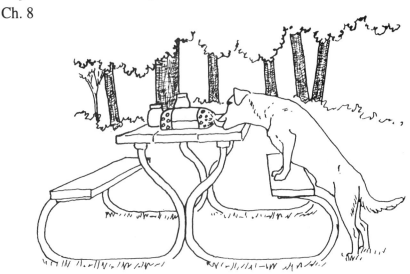

Many new faces had joined the beginning group by 1976. The membership tallied 725 members. Not only horses had taken to the forestlands, but motorcycles were being invented that could climb any hill, the steeper and sandier the better, and the new O.R.V.'s had been dreamt up for the non-horse, non-motorcycle person who wanted to explore the woods without walking. Both the federal and state governments were being bombarded with complaints from each group of rider, plus the private property owner was being disturbed by them all.

People were going into the woods with spray cans of paint and making trails anyplace they felt like making trails. The Forest Service had had enough of this splish-splashing of trees, so they set up some very strict criteria. The markings were to be every 1000 ft., a 4" circle of blue paint and a triangular marker 4 1/5 to 5 feet from ground level with aluminum nails. The trail was to be 6 feet wide, but only three in places, with 10 feet for heighth. The trails for the motorized toys would have their own color and markings.

The people who lived along the Manistee River were not happy with the river being torn up by horses swiming in the river and the debris floating downriver from the horses depositing their fecal matter in the waters. Other anti-environmental substances were being deposited in the rivers as well: shampoos, shaving creams, laundry detergents, dish detergents, bug sprays, petrochemical products, and just plain garbage that goes along with camping. There were rumors of the closing of

Goose Creek Camp.

There were always meetings to attend concerning all these matters. In the beginning things were so simple compared to what was happening now. There was no such thing as a simple horseback ride through the woods and rivers anymore. A horse was supposed to stay strictly on the marked trail. It was found that horses caused erosion on hills and turned a pathway way into deep sand. The trail along the AuSable had to be moved back away from the river because the hills had become so deeply cut into ravines. Some were so badly eroded that when you rode your horse down or up them, the banks were at the level of your horse's back. Jumping down the banks into the river was also tempting on a hot day. These places had to be fenced off and grass planted on the banks. A new trail from Luzerne to McKinley was made very twisty and turny to discourage motorcyclists. It turned out to be so bad, with so many logs across the trail, that even the horse people complained. Workbees had to be arranged to go in and clear out the trail. On the east side of the state, just south of Shecks, was a place called the onion farm. When it was sold to a new owner, he no longer allowed horses on his land. To get along beside it very mucky and dangerous. More workbees and meetings were called for. There always seemed to be problem about the use of the trail that had to be solved.

The good news was the Chamber of Commerce of Oscoda was trying to find a trail that would allow the horses to get to the shores of Lake Huron from Old Orchard Park.

"That Garn Bridge" was built at Ellis Lake the spring of 1977. Tony Wilhelm suggested it be named that in memory of Rex. It was a 45 foot span built by many of his friends, so it was a labor of love as well as a labor of necessity. The words, "That Garn Bridge" were routed right into the bridge's boards.

The June ride was another "double cross". Doc Lannen took on the job of Trail Boss. It was a long three weeks. Judy Schlink, a board member, took over for one day and Doc got to ride his horse to the next camp like a regular rider. He rode with two of his friends and it was a good refreshing ride.

Pat Worden took on the job for the fall ride. She had been trail boss in the past when the groups were smaller. She has some stories to tell about those earlier times. On one particularly hot summer day, a dog who was running along with his owners had collasped. She was told by some riders coming in that the dog was laying along the road at a certain place. She sent her husband, Wendy, out to pick up the dog with their truck and camper. When Wendy got there, the dog had revived itself by lopping into someone's soggy drainfield. Wendy didn't want him in the front, so · he did the next best thing; he put him in the camper. When he got back to camp and let the dog out, Pat couldn't believe the smell inside her camper. Pat slept outside that night. Wendy tried to clean up the camper.

Another time Wendy got himself into hot water was when he took off from camp, on his way to the next camp with the rig, and forgot their family cat. Pat had already ridden out with the riders. Sally heard the cat just a yowling and yowling,

86

looking for its rig. She went to investigate and couldn't find any sign of Wendy. She put the cat in their camper and sent him to the next camp in their rig. She caught up with Pat on the trail and told her what had happened to the cat. By the time Pat got into camp that night, she had simmered down to a low boil.

Besides taking care of yourself, a Trail boss has to know what is going on all over camp. He has to know who is registered for meals. He has to know who is registered for camping with the group. Sometimes when the trail ride gets into camp, other people are already camped there. If they become unruly and cause problems with the people on the trail ride, it is the Trail Boss's job to keep the peace in his group, but not the public. He can call for help from the board members that are present.

He also needs to know who has a stallion. Who has a little child. Who has a barking or troublesome dog. Who has camping experience or who doesn't. Who is a doctor. Who is a mechanic. Who is a farrier. Who is a veterinarian. Then there are the horses that escape nightly and are always found tied up at someone else's camp. Funny, how they stay tied at the other fellow's camp!

He also needs to know who knows the way to the next camp. The caravan has to move out at 8:00 a.m. every morning. Moving 225 rigs out of the campsites and onto the highways is a slow process, especially when the horses that aren't being ridden won't load. It works best when the caravans move in smaller groups, some moving as early as 6 a.m. He needs to know that the person leading those smaller caravans knows the way to the next camp.

When horses won't load, the trail boss has to wait to make sure the horse gets out of camp, one way or the other. Two different instances come to mind; The first was in 1975, on the fall ride. I was enjoying a very peaceful ride alone with my collie dog and my favorite Arabian mare. We were being held up by a stubborn palomino who had decided he was not going to get into his delapitated trailer. I watched about eight men try different tecniques that met with no success. Finally I walked over to the group and asked if I could try. About four of the men just walked off shrugging their shoulders. The owner of the horse gave me permission to try. I had the young man who seemed to be the most amiable to my plan, go inside the trailer and wrap the end of the lead rope around the most solid thing he could find. Then I tied a long rope to the braces by the fender of the trailer. I then wrapped it around the butt of the horse, not touching him with it, and brought it up around the fender brace on the other side of the trailer. I then handed it to two men and asked them to slowly pull the horse up the ramp and into the trailer. The horse saw us lift the rope up to wrap around his hindquarters and he ran up the ramp and into the trailer. We quickly raised the ramp and fastened it. The horse stood there quietly. I walked away not saying a word, actually a little disappointed that the horse had not let me prove my trailer loading abilities. I heard one of the men say that Rex told him if you ever needed help with a horse, just look for a woman camping alone with her horse. The second attempt at loading that comes to mind ended up with the girl riding

That Garn Bridge, 1977

That Garn Bridge

Convoy - June Ride, 1966

Building That Garn Bridge

her horse and the trail boss taking her back to get her rig later that day, after she arrived in camp.

If you went with an earlier group, the rides back to camp to get your horse were often on someone's lap, crammed in the back of someone else's pickup with his bed roll and bales of hay. You gave him a buck for gas and tried to remember what his rig looked like so you wouldn't get into that cramped-up position the next morning. After the kinks were out and you were on your horse, it didn't seem so bad. You got to meet a lot of people by jumping rigs. There was always a group riding back together who had stories to tell.

Another story told to me by Patty Basch was the time about 16 people were in the back of Bill Zettle's camper with at least three crammed on his bunk over his pickup cab. When they went around the corner from Supply Rd. onto U.S. 131 at South Boardman, the truck had a flat tire and almost tipped over into ditch on the right hand side of the road because it was so top heavy. I will leave the rest of the story for her to tell you!

Some member has to be the last one out of camp to inspect it for litter and make sure all the fires are out. The State of Michigan had found it necessary to require insurance and a bond to protect itself from being sued when people were hurt while playing on public lands. The bond was to protect the public lands from being destroyed by overzealous use and litter.

The Trail Boss has to get to the next camp before the last rig to help steer people into unknown parking places. People come who do not know how to back up their horse trailers. This can mean a big jam up and the exposure of bad tempers. More so if the weather is hot or pouring cold rain. If the weather is really hot, the Trail Boss makes the decision to have the riders leave early and have the shuttle truck run in the afternoon.

People are always losing things. There has to be a lost and found collection box at the Trail Boss's rig. Sometimes people get lost. Then the people who know the trail get back on their horses and use flashlights to go back down the trail to find the lost souls. Sometimes the people are hurt and really need them, other times they have just overestimated their horse or themselves and will be found sleeping in a soft place or leading their horse in.

In the beginning everyone brought their dogs and they ran loose with the kids. Then food started being stolen, and people were dumped off their horses when the dogs would go past on the trail and brush their legs. Evelyn Broegman remembers taking two people to the hospital for just that reason. Finally the rules had to be made to keep dogs on a leash at all times. One other thing that dogs do that is very irritating, is lift their legs on saddles waiting to be put on horse's backs. There is no better way to make an enemy than to let your dog whiz on someone else's equipment while it is sitting on the ground.

The third edition of the guidebook was printed in 1977. It was a smaller version of the old one, with the maps made singularly on a coated, thick paper that

90

repelled water. They folded up to the size of a saddle bag, and were all kept in a plastic folder of the same measurements. Phyllis Garn and Doc Lannen deserve the credit for the up-grading and printing of the new book and maps. The art work was again donated by Duane "Bud" Weert.

Bob Broegman tackled the job of trail boss in 1977 and has been guiding the trail rides every year since then. (1995) For thirty-one years Bob has spent his Junes and Octobers either riding or helping others ride the Michigan Riding and Hiking Trail across the state of Michigan. He has done a lot of work and seen a lot of changes. He handles it very well.

On the June ride of 1977, a virus hit the horses. They would run high temperatures and then get runny noses and coughs. The group decided to have everyone take their horse's temperature every morning. If the horse did not have a fever, he could be ridden. I saw Jane McGuinn tip-toe in bare feet out to her horse when she first got up in the morning. She inserted the thermometer and clipped it to the horse's tail. She then went back into her camper and made breakfast. When she came out to check the horse, she could not find the thermometer. She rode the horse anyway, and all day people kidded her about her horse swallowing his thermometer.

A new public address system was purchased in 1977, just in time to save Four Mile Camp from burning. It was late in the afternoon, after most of the horses were in camp, that someone discovered a fire just to the south of the camp. The wind was blowing it right toward camp. The call for help came over the P.A. System and people responded immediately with shovels, blankets, buckets of water, and anything they could find to put out the fire. It was burning in the Jack Pines and jumping from treetop to treetop. We managed to hold it until the D.N.R. could get there with big equipment. It was facinating to watch them push down trees and dig ditches with their big trucks. It was never known how the fire got started, but we realized that we would not have been able to evacuate all the rigs in time to save them.

Another tragic thing happened at Four Mile Camp that I had to bad fortune to witness. A rider came running in and said that a horse was down a few miles back up the trail toward Grayling in a very sandy part of the trail. A group of people took off to rescue it with a two-horse trailer and a pickup. The next thing we spectators saw was a horse being hauled back into camp held up in the trailer by ropes. The poor thing was unable to stand because of something broken in one front leg. The men wanted to have the horse put down but the girl who owned it could not part with it. They ended up hauling it all the way to Michigan State University Veterinary Hospital by slinging it with ropes and blankets used as straps, only to be told the animal could not be saved. This accident was not the fault of the rider, it was deemed caused by the deep sand and maybe something weak in the horse's bones.

The trail was being changed from Four Mile to a new camp south of Luzerne up in the hardwoods. They would no longer use Hardy Camp. The trail east out of Luzerne would now cross a huge swamp with the East Branch of Big Creek and a smaller swamp outlet (a drain within a swamp) that needed bridges and the rest

91

of the area being too soft for horses needed a boardwalk a 1/4 mile long. The brige across the main creek was built by the Forest Service as a Youth Conservation corps project in 1978. The other smaller span and the boardwalk were built by the Forest Service as a Young Adult Conservation Corps project in 1978 also. The trail riders worked on the guard rails and slippery floor. They ended up putting down snowmobile treads for grippers. The trail riders dubbed it "Whatta Bridge". It is about four miles east of Luzerne Camp. There is a place to get a cold drink where the water is piped out of a spring and runs into a trough at the east end of the bridge.

The camp, itself, is a cool camp under the big leaves of the hardwoods. It has a large camping area that is open by permit only. This permitted area has 29 units with spur parking and 18 pull-throughs that make up 36 units in the over flow area. There are 10 units with spurs that are open to the public without permits.

The pump at Luzerne left a lot to be desired. It was (is) very deep and took about 25 pumps to even get the water to the top and then it came in cupfuls. For a big organized ride, the Luzerne Fire Department would bring up water in their fire trucks and dump it into large tanks. This method was used for years until a deep water well was put in that worked off a generator in the overflow area. This camp was first used in 1979. The trail to the east, to McKinley camp, was the new one I mentioned that was so twisty-turny that motorcyclists didn't like it.

By 1979 the Forest Service felt that the rides should have only about 200 to 250 riders to ease the adverse impacts on the trail by so many horses at one time. Because the group (at that time) had nothing in the by-laws limiting how many people could attend the rides, the Forest Service tried to limit the numbers by making camps that would accomodate only that number. The officers met this request by increasing the number of rides and therefore dispersing the number of riders on the trail and in the camps over the season. They decided to put on a September ride. This ride was scheduled for the middle of the month and most of the time went all the way across Michigan in 10 days. This seemed to fit the bill for many riders who loved to ride as much as they could and the time of year was certainly great for that.

In 1980 the DNR decided to put camping fees on all the camps on state land. This meant more meetings which finally ended with the resolution of the group paying a one time fee for each camp.

This year they also camped in Old Orchard Park for the first time. Their trail into Lake Huron took them to AuSable, a town connected by growth, to Oscoda. It is basically a snowmobile trail.

In 1982, a school bus was purchased for the shuttle back to camp. The DNR closed Hopkins Creek, Clam River and Elk Hill.

In 1983, a new trail from Goose Creek to Four Mile Camp meant riding through army manuvers. This made the first part very exciting. The second part, west of Grayling and east of Lake Margarethe, across M-72 was a mouse act trying to get through the maze of blue trails to Four Mile Rd. Once there, it was a simple matter of committing hari-cari going over the via duct across I-75 on a horse.

92

There was also a new trail from South Branch Camp to Lake Huron that year. It is an easy trail, but a little boring. No views or rivers, in fact there isn't anyplace to drink the whole day. Cool and safe though, through pines and scrub oak.

They also put a new deep water pump in the Goose Creek campground back in the open area. There already is a good hand pump there, for people who do not have generators.

1984 saw many workbees. There was always something that needed to be done to a campground or some part of the trail to keep it up.

South Branch camp was closed Oct. 1, 1985. In order to use the camp there, a written application must be submitted 14 days previous to the date requested with payment of the permit and use fees. Deep water wells were put in at Kalkaska, Luzerne and McKinley that year.

Luzerne Bridge, 1983

Bob Broegman on Luzerne Bridge, 1983

AND THE TRAIL RIDES GO ON
Ch.9

By 1985 all of the original group have faded into the background of the organization. There are over 1000 members now and the problems of keeping the trail and camps open are never ending. Doc Lannen and Phyllis Garn have held in there the longest, except for Bob Broegman, who continues to guide the trail rides from point to point. It's like a natural phenomenom with him now, like birds that fly north in the spring and south in the winter.

Some have been given Honorary Memberships which means they do not have to pay their yearly dues to stay members. These people are; Fred Haskins, Fitch Williams, Rex Garn, Phyllis Garn, Russell "Bud" Weaver, Anthony Wilhelm, Sally Wilhelm, Harold Babbit, and Richard "Doc" Lannen.

1985 was a year without a caterer again. Now it takes a lot of planning to be able to eat for two weeks without going to a grocery store. Most of the people only had ice chests. At the beginning of the ride you could eat steaks and hamburger and by the end of it the menu would be canned stew or fish. Deep water wells were put in at Kalkaska Camp, Luzerne Camp and McKinley for generators. Other workbees were at Goose Creek and Shecks. Nearly $16,000.00 was spent on the trail this year from organization money, not counting the volunteer labor by the members.

In 1986 they decided to try another ride to cut down on the large attendance that was plaguing the DNR and The Forest Service. This one was to be in the first part of May. They called it the "Blossom Ride". It was a success.

High Banks of AuSable

Alcona Pond - AuSable River 1966
Bob Broegman, Lee Stump & Dana Lannen

In 1987 the group tackled the job of building a new bridge across Big Creek just east of Luzerne Camp. (The one dubbed "Whatta Bridge" earlier, but that name never caught on. It became known as "The Luzerne Bridge".) The old one had rotted and horses were breaking boards and falling through while crossing. Most people were taking the alternate route around. The workbee was planned for nine days; May 2 until May 10. It would be the biggest work detail they had ever attempted. The Forest Service would remove the old bridge with the help of two prison crews, and would be there with the big equipment to help bring in the lumber for the new one. The F.S. was to provide 230 6"x8"x8" pressure treated mud sills, 690 pieces of 1/4" x 12" rod and 21 boxes of #60 pole barn spikes.

The organization ordered 345 pieces of 3"x5"x10' stringers and 2760 pieces of 3"x5"x6' all made out of oak and double pressure treated. It would cost the organization $14,682.00 in money and 2,760 man hours. They started after the board meeting on Thursday and by the next Tuesday afternoon it was done. Doc Lannen remembers it well because when they had finished they all sat down to have a beer. Bill Zettel offered Doc some salted peanuts and Doc said "sure". A few hours after he had eaten them he had a terrible attack of divirticulitus and ended up in the hospital. He was especially upset because the following week after the bridge building was a trail ride for buggies and he had planned to attend it. As it was, he made the last few days.

The DNR had opened Elk Hill again when they found that people were going to use that camp. So in 1987, the fall ride rode from Elk Hill to Shecks.

In 1988 they put a well in at Elk Hill. It cost the group $1,600.00. Just a hand pump, but it worked great and the water was delicious.

There were many other accomplishments in 1988; A new deep well at the Gerry Lake Overflow on top of the hill. That cost about $2500.00. Rebuilt "That Garn Bridge". Worked on the trail to Cadillac. The FS had to remove the pump handles from McKinley and Luzerne Camps. People were oiling the sqeaking parts and the oil had contaminated the water. Bob Broegman along with other board members worked on the one at Luzerne and after "millions" of gallons of water were pumped from the well by generator, it was deemed fit for drinking once again.

In 1988, it was decided that any horses coming to the rides from other states would need health certificates and negative coggins tests. Judy Schlink lost her beautiful Arabian gelding to Swamp Fever just a few months after she had ridden on the June Ride the year before. She and Margaret Stanton had to watch him get sicker and sicker until he had to be destroyed.

The big job of this year would be making McKinley Camp a circle camp. This meant another big workbee because many rows of Jack Pine had to be cut down, and stumps removed making it possible for rigs to drive a full circle. It was considered a fire trap the way it was in the past.

The Upper Manistee River Association was complaining to the DNR about the misuse of the river again. The sand that is stirred up by the horses fills in around

AuSable River, 1968

Gerry Lake Camp, 1967

he stones leaving nowhere for the fish eggs to hold until they hatch. It was decided to improve the approach to the river on the east side. It was to be made of cement with steps for the horses to negoiate.

The world is starting to learn what a fragile thing our ecosystem really is. Horse people ruin rivers for fishermen. Horse people ruin hiking paths for hikers. Horse people dirty up city streets when our horses choose that time to deficate. Horse people make motorcyclists mad because they complain about bikers scaring horses.

I made a cyclist so mad one day he chased me with his bike. It was over on the Blue Trail about half-way between Goose Creek and Bear Lake. I was heading east on a competitive trail ride so I was riding for time. I came up behind three men astraddle their bikes pushing them up a small sandy grade. I followed them a ways and tried to make them hear me. Finally I just told my horse to go for it and pass them. There were banks on both sides and as we passed the first biker, he yelled and my horse spooked and jumped up on the bank on the brush. We kept on going and passed the second one. By the time I passed the third one I was in a full gallop. He didn't hear me coming and I scared him going by so fast. He screamed at me that he was going to kill me. The adenaline starting pumping in me and my horse and we ran the last four miles to the road just outside of Goose Creek Camp. I looked back right after I passed and he was trying to get up that sandy incline as fast as he could. My girlfriend, who was riding a bay horse behind me, came upon the same group and was told to tell me if he ever saw me again, he was going to shoot that —————horse right out from underneath me. At first he thought she was me and he was really puffed up and mad. She, being a confident female, was not intimidated by his size and informed him in no uncertain terms that she was not the person whom he was seeking. I thought it was sorta funny that the shoe was on the other foot for once.

The bridge at South Branch eroded in 1989 and was torn out. The Forest Service planned to build another one at the cost of $10,000.00. Meanwhile the people were to go to McKinley the old way by crossing the South Branch of the AuSable and following the AuSable. The most beautiful way in my opinion.

In 1990, because of a waiver that has to be signed by anybody wanting a membership, agreeing that they have read the guidebook and understand all the rules, it was decided that a person would have to be a member for 30 days before a trail ride. This would allow ample time to read this book. These problems were brought on by overzealous court cases from people hurt on state or federal lands.

There was also a change in the by-laws concerning new memberships. Any person who wants to join has to have the approval of the majority of the board of directors. Once the application is submitted to the secretary, it is on hold until a board of directors meeting.

In 1990, the South Branch bridge was completed. The final cost was $15,000.00. This was all paid for by the Forest Service.

By 1991 there were approximately 1,350 members. There was a lot to do

Bob Walters - 1987 - New Luzerne Bridge

1987 - Luzerne Bridge Crew at work

that year: South Branch needed four new toilets; They needed a camp in the Cadillac Area; Walker Road Trail Camp needed a hand pump and a john; Goose Creek was to get a new deep well pump; Sheck's also needed two more toilets; A bridge needed to be built over Hoppy Creek between McKinley and South Branch; Four Mile Camp needed campsite improvement; McKinley Camp needed two more johns and more parking area cleared. Workbees were scheduled and members obliged.

In 1992 a new bridge was built on the road over the West Branch of Big Creek by the Roscommon Road Commission. This proved to be a problem with the trail riders because it was the last place to water just four miles out of Luzerne Camp especially since the well was so deep and so seldom used the leathers would dry up and pumping was an effort in futility. After a meeting with the Road Commission, the Forest Service, and the organization, it was concluded that a trail could be made into the river where it used to be, with certain criteria that would prevent erosion to the bank.

The township of AuSable was objecting to people using their park to unload horses and ride them into Lake Huron. Too much manure was being left for other people to step in when coming to the park. The horse people were put on probation.

This type of thing is so hard to control. If you are a member of the organization, you will get the newsletters and have knowledge of these problems. If you are just a horse owner that wants to ride from shore to shore and when you get to Lake Huron and find you can't start in the water, it is quite upsetting.

The Pigeon River Country caretakers were getting upset with horse people riding on the hiking pathways. Also people at elk viewing areas were complaining about horse people riding out in front of them so they couldn't see the elk.

The 1992 June ride registered 410 with 330 at one camp. The dust conditions in camp with this many people is constant. Any rig that drives by, or horse that is led by, stirs up dust that blows in the campers. With so many riders on the trail, dust was a problem there also.

Beavers had caused a problem on Wilbur Creek near the Curtisville store. The dam caused the back waters to flood the trail and close a bridge. Another beaver dam on Hoppy Creek about 4 miles west of South Branch caused a problem on the bridge. Work bees were planned to go into the wilds and solve these problems.

By 1995 the group was not allowed to cross Smith Bridge between Luzerne and Four Mile Camps. By user groups working together, a temporary military bridge was laid on top of the old bridge, with new decking and gravel for approaches it was again useable.

This year also brought about the culmination of a new trail from Elk Hill to Luzerne camp. A much more scenic trail with two more beautiful camps. A 16 foot bridge had to be built over the spillway at Stoney Creek. Wet spots had to be filled in. Corner posts and trail marker posts had to be planted.

The handful of people who started this trail 32 years ago still stand by and watch over it. They always care no matter where they live or for whatever health reasons they don't ride anymore. The first small group worked in their spare time to create a beautiful pathway across Michigan from shore to shore. The large group that has the care of it today surely has their hands full. They spend their time trying to keep it. Hopefully they can hold on to it so the grandchildren and great grandchildren have some place to ride their horses to get away from it all.

Grave of local man near McKinley Camp

? - Tony Wilhelm - Rex Garn - Fred Stackable - Joyce Franks

Mud Lake Camp, 1967

Shecks Camp, 1968

BUGGY RIDES ON THE TRAIL
Ch. 10

It all started in 1985. Doc's friends, Ted and Jane McManus, acquired a team of Morgan's and a buggy. Doc, not wealthy in money, only health and energy, was given a pile of steel that he thought looked like junk, but the giver said it was a buggy. In this pile was one recognizable part: the springs. Doc started to research old books and catalogs for buggy pictures that would be clear enough for him to tell how to build a buggy with the framework that was supposedly in that pile of junk.

He eventually found a book that had fifty buggies in it and he found the springs that matched the ones he had. He now had a project. Through the winter months he was busy building his buggy from just this one picture. It turned out to be a two seater, wooden box with a foam rubber cushion covered with cloth for a seat, and wooden spoked wheels with hard rubber tires. (He bought the wheels and the old buggy pull.)

This project was taking Doc back in time, because he was brought up on a farm driving his dad's grade Percherons (one bay and one black) to do the farm work. Now he would have his own dappled gray Arabians to drive.

Word got around about Doc's buggy and people started showing up that also had the same interests and some form of wagon pulled by horses. They put together a plan to drive their buggies/wagons across Michigan as close to the Michigan Riding and Hiking Trail as possible in the spring of 1986.

Bill Plamondon (a very staunch member of The Michigan Trail Riders

Association) helped them find the two tracks that would network them across the state.

In the spring of 1986, five couples trucked their wagons and horses to Oscoda, Mi and after getting their horses' feet wet in Lake Huron (traditional for MTRA people) started west. Only 136 years behind their forefathers.

The group included:

Doc and Jean in their homemade open top buggy, pulled by two Arabians.

Ted and Jane McManus, in their new piano box with a folding blacktop, pulled by two Morgans.

Terry and Jackie Lautner, in an ordinary narrow flat farm wagon with rubber tires. He had made steel bows that held a big orange canvas and he pulled it with a team of Belgians. He looked like a real pioneer.

Leonard and Carol Lautner (Terry's Uncle) had a buggy frame with a box and cover. He pulled it with one Quarter Horse.

The only people who were not from the Traverse City area were George and Marion Robbins from Mooretown, Ontario. They had an ordinary piano box buggy with hard rubber tires (patented in 1890) on wooden spoked wheels with a blacktop pulled by a Quarter Horse.

They used the regular MTRA campgrounds. Being raised in modern times with modern conviences, these people faired better than their ancestors; they brought along their motor homes or pickup campers. This modern accessory meant they had to take it to the next camp every morning and drive back to their horses and buggies. Their day started early and ended late. It also rained 5 of the days and Doc remembers it well because he had the only uncovered rig. Now everyone goes covered.

All five couples made it to Empire in good shape. Terry Lautner's dad made them all a nice wooden trophy signifying a wagon and the blue trail.

All these couples had a least one dog. The dogs loved to ride in the wagons. They either sat in the seats or watched the scenery from the floor on a good day when the covers were rolled back.

The group went again in 1987, but Doc had a bout of illness and missed the first three days. (This is mentioned in the chapter that tells about building the new Luzerne Bridge.) He had a different buggy this time; it had a top.

Buggies do not need a license, but they do need those slow moving vehicle signs to be used on the roads legally.

Today, ten years later, there are about the same number in the group, but different people. Health problems have interfered with their fun. They have also discontinued trying to go across the state. There were some near traffic accidents, because the people of today who drive cars and trucks do not realize that horses can be frightened by them. They were crowded on bridges where they did not have any choice but to gallop to get across. To gallop a team of horses, on slick pavement,

106

being passed by trucks and cars was a bit more excitement than they wanted. They have a lot more peace and quiet just driving in the woods and on the back roads.

The women were getting tired of the weather. It got so every rainy day, they would go ahead to the next town and go shopping all day.

Over the years, Doc has built eight buggies. He has found two people who have been very helpful to him. Bill Baese, a retired house builder from Prudenville, who devotes all his time to building buggies, and George Moss, Mt Pleasant, who repairs the buggies from Mackinaw Island and even out of the state. He has two girls that work for him. One does upholstery and the other builds the tops. He has every kind of part.

There are a lot of people who like to drive teams of horses. Doc has met a lot of new people since he started building buggies. He does it just for himself. When he gets a bug to make one, he just sells his old one and builds a new one.

Ted and Jane McManus, two of his best friends, have a big driving arena at South Boardman and teach people how to drive horses. Jane is a judge for driving classes at horse shows.

There is a growing interest in driving a horse while it is pulling a buggy. Quite often you will see organized buggy rides around the camps that are located in the less populated areas. It is fun, but it can also be dangerous. If you happen to see some covered wagons, give them a little space and then wave slowly so you won't spook the horses.

Doc Lannen ~ Bo and Vega

Leona & Phyllis with Bud's chuck wagon

Leona Riecha

COOKING FOR THE TRAIL RIDES
Ch. 11

Through the eyes of a trail rider I always saw the chuck wagon as a place to wander over to catch up on the latest "goings on" because it seemed like someone was always there, either munching or sipping on something. Leona was always there preparing something good for the next meal. She sorta adopted us all and looked out for us.

The more I thought about this cook shack always being there, with tarps flapping in the wind, rain, or sleet, I got to wondering how they managed to feed so many people, day after day, in the woods, far away from any modern convenience. Joe passed away a few years ago, but Leona still lives in their home in Traverse City where she is visited daily by at least one of their five sons and their children. She said she would tell me how it was to cook in the woods far away from home.

Exerpts from Leona's memories; "This is my first attempt at writing, but Rhoda talked me into a chapter.

"In the summer of 1974, I met two gentlemen at Dill's where I worked as a waitress. (I should say high pressure salesmen!) Tony Wilhelm and a man known as Rex. They asked if Joe and I would be interested in catering the trail ride in October. No newcomers to cooking, but absolute green horns to what else we were getting into, we decided to give it a whirl. We soon learned it wasn't going to be a joy-ride.

"Our first job took us north to Elk Hill that fall the first week of October.

The tap had been left open on the water tank of the chuck wagon so we had no water. There weren't any johns for us city folks. We got delayed on our way to camp so the 101 dinners were not prepared for the unsuspecting hungry riders. It was rainy and cold and we had to be sure to follow Big Red to the next camps. Because of the mud, Rex skipped Babbitts Ranch and went straight to Goose Creek. Things were better there.

"Each morning we were up at least by 5 o'clock to serve breakfast by six. We learned to break camp by 8 o'clock so we could follow Rex to the next camp. Because we arrived with the big group, it was not easy getting near the pump. Everyone wanted near the pump and even though it was a known fact that the cooks needed water, it seemed like it was always a struggle. Mike (one of the five sons who took turns going along and helping) said he got pretty good at backing up the chuck wagon into some tight places. Once in camp the tarps had to be rigged so they wouldn't blow down, which they seemed always destined to. Two cooking ranges had to be unloaded from the chuck wagon and set up along side and hooked up to the gas pig. Four big heavy tables also had to be unloaded from the chuck wagon and set up. Then the evening meal had to be started.

"The chuck wagon had two refrigerators with freezers that held the noon lunch meats. They were gas and very tempermental; The chuck wagon had to be exactly level for them to work right, and then the wind would find the pilot and blow out the flame. The other food was kept in big ice chests. Joe had his contacts in Traverse city where he could get good cuts of meat, and quality food, (he was very picky about his food) but making trips to Traverse city from the other side of the state was costly. He tried to find good meats when on the east side, but would quite often be unhappy with what he got.

"Each ride seemed to take us into the unknown with the taking of wrong turns and so forth. Once Rex was leading the carvan to Trails End and he took a wrong turn. All the rigs got stuck in the mud.

"We needed two pulling vehicles; One to pull the chuck wagon and the other to pull our sleeping quarters. These vehicles were always stuffed with food. We burned the clutch out of a van at Shecks, drove through mud up to the bottom of the vehicles between 4 Mile and Hardy's, had a flat tire on the chuck wagon on the ramp of I-75 on the way to 4 Mile, had a flat tire on the way out of Goose creek, and had another one on the camper on the way from Luzerne to McKinley.

"We could only plan for two days at a time so Joe had to go back to Traverse City every other day. One evening after dinner he took off for home on a trip that should have taken 2 1/2 hours at the most and headed north instead of west, got lost way north somewhere and finally got back to Traverse in the wee hours of the morning. Needless to say each trip got easier as we learned the route.

"Each year meant a different towing vehicle so that meant rewiring the light hook-ups.

"We always tried to be in bed by 10 o'clock each night, which was not easy.

110

I remember always being tired and not having enough time. The first double cross from shore to shore and back again, I think I cried every night. I got so tired the least little thing would upset me. By the end of that trip I was a total disaster.

"Getting help was very hard. Teenagers did not want to work that hard so we had to count on our sons. Mike, Pat, Tim, Brian and Greg would take turns. Joe's brother Julian and wife Dorothy went on one ride to help drive and were a great help with all the other work like setting up. Even talked Hunce Martineau into going once. At least 4 people were needed to make everything go right.

"One time at McKinley camp, my help decided to ride back to Traverse with Jim Curtis. They said they would be back sometime during the night, but didn't make it. Doc Lannen and Pat Worden started flipping flapjacks and were a great help with breakfast that morning. All I had to do was ask and I got the help I needed. Joe worked his regular job on some of our trips.

"Once there was a fire a half mile back of the camp at 4 Mile. Brian was the only one with a truck loose from hook-up. He was bare footed, but grabbed a broom and rake from the chuck wagon and people jumped in the back and headed out. By the time the fire fighters got there, the trail riders had it pretty well under control.

"At Goose Creek I got up early as usual, and heard a horse in trouble. I grabbed a butcher knife and cut the lead line that was tangled around his legs and he got up. I never thought about getting hurt at the time, even though I knew nothing about horses.

"Seems like we were always jump starting vehicles for people.

"We did meet a lot of nice people and would look forward to seeing them each year. We only had complaints on our food once and that was from some people from Canada who didn't like our canned vegetables."

After reading Leona's notes, it occured to me that they were there with a job to do. We were all there because we got to ride our horses all day. To cook a meal for 2 or 4 people at night was fun, but I can imagine cooking for 100 people every day would have been a real challenge, especially the kind of banquets the Reichas prepared.

111

In the Water at Empire

The AuSable River

TRAIL TALES
Ch. 12

    In this chapter is a collection of stories that happened along the trails that are true and need to be included in this history book.

    One time Pat Worden and Sally Wilhelm were marking the trail from Goose Creek out to Meyers Rd. They came across a bunch of signs for a motorcycle race. Sally said, "I'll fix those guys," and she turned the signs in another direction. They never did hear any motorcycles so they guessed the race must have been scheduled for another day. They really wished they could have seen the faces on those motorcyclists when they came upon those wrong way signs. As the story goes, they had been restricted to a walk on the way out, stopping every little way to mark a tree, being sure both sides of a corner showed the user the correct way through the maze of trails in the area. It is a distance of about 8 miles and they were looking forward to having a nice canter on the way back. They had just gotten down to the bottom of the first hill when they came across a girl on a really fancy horse with a brand new expensive saddle. It had silver all over it and a name in silver across the back making them think the girl was really some rider to have a saddle like that. The girl asked if she could ride back to camp with them. Sally said, "Yeh, but we're going to move right along." At that Pat and Sally lifted into the canter. They immediately heard a terrified scream from behind. The girl yelled out, "I've never ridden a horse at a dead run like this before." Pat looked back and the girl had dropped her reins and was hanging onto the horn with both hands. They all ended up walking all the way back. They learned not to pick up new riders after that.

A short cut found Jane McGuinn and Pat Worden along a river bank that had eroded so badly only the sod was holding a shelf along the edge. There was a bog on the other side. Pat got off her horse and led him so he could get close to the trees and not bang her legs. She expected any time to go through the sod. She looked back and saw Jane off her horse. When Jane caught up she said, "Don't you ever tell anyone that I got off my horse, we just don't do that." When Pat got into camp that night she yelled out so everyone could hear, "Hey Sally, Jane got off her horse and led it today."

One time, a small group was riding through the birches. Amy Wilhelm was riding her small horse Specky in the lead. Whoever was second got too close and Specky kicked up his heels. Amy fell off the front of the horse and everybody cantered over her and never hurt her.

Pat Worden was thrown off her horse on an embankment on the AuSable River when a combination of a runaway horse and a person passing her horse put Pat's horse in a tizzy and Pat fell off over his shoulder. She fell on her shoulder and put it out of place. They tied it up to her chest with a bandana and two belts and she rode on into camp.

One day, when Sally was riding with Ginny Franklin, Ginny's daughter MaLissa, Tony, and Fred Stackable, coming into Lost Creek Sky Ranch, there was a 3 1/2 foot barricade on the road ahead. Ginny and MaLissa did a lot of jumping so they ran toward it and cleared it with no problem. Sally made a quick sachet around and Tony was right behind her. Sally turned around just in time to see Fred go up and over it. He never leaned forward or anything and old Bingo went right over that thing. He was still on him and he didn't even look surprised or anything. A little ways further down the trail, he said, "That was pretty neat, I've never jumped on a horse before."

One year over by South Branch, there were a lot of trees down on the trail. Bob Barlow was our eldest rider of that time, somewhere in his late 70's. He was a retired General Motors engineer from Lansing. He was very hard of hearing, but a very fine gentleman. He became a member of the board of directors of MTRA. He always rode alone. Tony and Sally were riding along and saw Bob's horse along by the trees. Tony said, "Let's ride up there." So they did and saw him just lying there. They were just sure he had keeled over and was dead. They called out, "Bob, Bob". He picked up his head and said, "I wish you people would let me sleep, everybody keeps going by and waking me up." He lived a few years more, but did pass away at home getting ready for a trail ride. He was 80.

It had become a tradition for Pat and Sally to spend some time in the bar at Empire before a big crossing. This particular time they had promised to get back to their campers early so as not to start the ride with a hangover. When they started back, they saw a person coming toward them that would encourage them to go back, so they stepped into the bushes along the side of the sidewalk. Pat immediately stepped into something gooey and the further she went into it, the deeper it got. It was up over her knees and thick. She tried to get Sally to help her out, but neither had a flashlight. Sally took one step and decided to back out. Pat tried to run and fell into the stuff flat on her face. She crawled on her belly to get out of it and they made it back to Sally's camper where Sally got a flashlight. When she shone it on Pat, she said, "Pat, you are coated with some terrible gray stuff and you can't come into my camper like that." About that time a friend of Pat's from Traverse City drove in and saw her. They decided to go over to the 50 gallon barrel full of horse water and clean up. Pat stripped off her clothes and jumped into the water tank. Then she had to run across the lot, in the dark, really fast, to her camper, where she had a clean set of clothes. They later learned that what she fell into was the foundation for the vault of the bank that was being built there. They never told anybody whose body print was in that cement. They rode past in the next morning and the men who came to trowel off the cement were going beserk at the mess they had to work with. Sally and Pat just looked at each other and rode on past.

Sally Wilhelm remembers a humorous situation they found themselves in when they went about "stealing" outhouses; "In the early years some of our camps had no toilet facilities, so the Conservation Department (now the DNR) offered us old outhouses that were being replaced with new ones in some of the State Campgrounds - - - if we would remove them ourselves. That sounded good to us. Jim Sutton worked for Rennie Oil company and was able to use their stake truck that had a hydraulic lift tailgate. Now, Jim didn't ride but his wife Barb (now Barb Weaver) did, and having been involved with the trail since it's conception, they were used to being called out for work-bees. On our very first toilet excursion we arrived at the busy campground and Jim proceeded to back the truck up to the outhouse. People started coming from all directions, wanting to know what we were doing with their toilets. I still don't know if they thought we were stealing them, but when we got to the last one, a guy ran up and said, 'Please, not to take it until he had a chance to use it.' I don't remember how many trips we made, but we were able to supply outhouses for Jim Hardy's Camp behind Lost Creek Sky Ranch, the old Luzerne Camp, Stewart Creek Camp (these two camps were on Consumers Power property) and Jackson Creek crossing (an intermediate camp)."

Jane McGuinn rode her big horse Anne into the landing at Smith Bridge one year, and the horse just fell over onto the ground. Rex stuck his finger on her eye and it just stared at them. He mixed up some salt in a coke bottle and got it into her and the horse stood back up and was able to go on.

When Doc Lannen first started trail riding they purchased a homemade two wheeled trailer. He was able to get a friend to put another axle under it, making it more stable. It did not have a manger, but had a breast board for the horses to lean against. At that time they had a friendly donkey who liked to be with the horses. They could put him in the manger area and he would ride crossways of the trailer without undue harassment from the horses. One summer evening they trailered out to McFaddens who lived next to the State Game Area. When they arrived they picketed the horses and Flash, the donkey. They started out riding, Jean on Gypsy and Doc on Jerry. Mac and Bernice McFadden and Roy and Clara Hayes completed the party. As they left Mac asked if Doc wasn't going to take Flash. Doc said he thought he'd be a nuisance and would probably get lost. Mac finally talked Doc into turning the donkey loose. Flash trudged along behind until they turned around to go back. It was dark by then and they were riding single file. Doc was riding out in front and as the ones in back could not hear him very well, he had turned around and was riding backwards in the saddle. Jerry did not mind and would follow the trail. Doc had brought along a big lantern and had that in his hands. Suddenly Flash realized that he had been left behind. He went cantering past them all toward camp. Doc thinks he whispered something to Jerry about a race, because Jerry took off at a canter right after him. Doc could not find the reins and ended up on the ground. Jean came along on Gypsy and they rode back double. They must have been a sight, Doc riding on back with a flashlight looking for his horse. Soon Gypsy nickered and Jerry answered. It wasn't any trouble catching him and they rode back without further incident. A quote from Doc's memoirs, "Sometimes it does not pay to show off!"

Doc remembers the year Mr. Corwin died and they didn't use the Corwin farm for a camp. The people had to go on a ways farther to the South Branch Ranch. The sign was confusing and many people rode on by. One couple kept going until dark and came to the conclusion that they were lost. They flagged down a motorist and their conclusion was confirmed. The man hitched a ride back to the ranch to get his trailer. When he got back to the horses, the lady's horse would not get in. He went back to the ranch for help and on the way back, noticed he was low on gas. When he finally got some gas from a gas station that had closed and gone to bed, he continued on his way to get the horse. When he finally went to dinner, it was midnight. Lost people were a common occurrence on the first trail rides.

One fall ride when it was so bitter cold, Tony and Sally remember crawling into their down sleeping bags and then heard some noise outside their makeshift camper. They saw some people taking hay and sprinkling it around the fire and then putting their sleeping bags on it and crawling in. It was very close to the fire so Tony warned them that if the hay should catch fire, they would be trapped in their sleeping bags. One of them said, "Yeh, but we'd at least be warm for a little while."

Doc liked to take people out for circle rides and pretend he was lost. One time he was leading a group out of Goose Creek to the north. One of the men said his horse wouldn't cross the river. Doc said that he would tell him how to get back to camp. He said fine, then he could go along. When Doc crossed the river, there was the man. Doc said, "I thought your horse wouldn't cross rivers?" The man said, "I didn't either, but when the rest went, the old ——just went with em." There were two dentist's wives who had never crossed the river before either. They all seemed to have such a good time at it, Doc went up river a way and crossed again. Then Doc

116

let another fellow take the lead for awhile and he ended up getting them into a cul-de-sac. Doc pulled out his compass and the looks on the faces were shear panic. They were sure he would never get them back to camp. He knew which way he wanted to go, but he would have to circle to get there.

In the fall of 1964, while Doc and Jean were going through Clare, they were pulled over to the curb. The officer asked them if they had any hay or straw on board. Doc said he did. The officer said he would have to relieve him of it because he was leaving a quarantined area for the cereal leaf beetle. The officer took all his horse food. Luckily, in those days, Rex always had plenty of hay in the back of his stock truck.

That same day Doc and Jean met the riders going into camp and Rex was leading a pack horse. Because they had only 24 people registered for this fall ride, there wasn't any catering. Rex asked Doc to go back to town and get some food for supper that night. Luckily, they had met up with Doc. It's nice to have friends out in the woods!

Tony tells of his wild ride on Honey Pot. "Years back, I rode a prancy, fidgety mare named 'Honey Pot'. Les Botimer rode a beautiful, big Appaloosa stallion. He liked to hassle my mare by buzzing past me and making her bolt to catch him. This one time we were approaching Smith Bridge from the east. The trail is quite winding through there and when he approached from behind, I was just sitting peacefully with my reins hanging loose, enjoying the quiet. Of course Honey Pot bolted and the devil got ahold of me and I just let her go full speed ahead. I was not aware that a tornado had been through there and when we rounded one of those sharp curves there were trees all across the trail. Honey Pot and I were way ahead of Les by this time and she just leaped those trees with me hanging on. I didn't see Les for about a half an hour after that. He must have gotten tangled up in that tree mess, but he never would admit it."

For some reason I have not been able to figure, quite severe weather patterns would cross over the Mio - Luzerne area. There are two times that left severe impressions on my mind. The first one occurred at Hardy Camp on the June Ride. We were coming from the west and as we crossed the airport we saw a bank of big black clouds hanging low over camp. The wind picked up and the thunder and lightening started. We (Roger, I, and five children we had taken across that year.) hurried into camp, unsaddled as fast as we could and threw the saddles in a pile in the four horse trailer. We had just gotten our horses tied to the picket lines when it broke loose. The hail beat down on the horses and they lunged this way and that trying to find comfort. We finally tucked their heads under our bodies and held them tight by the halters. It piled up on the leaves about 8 to 10 inches deep. It blew into our open pick-up cap and the open sided horse trailer and soaked our sleeping bags. I remember Doc Lannen remarking that he had picked up the ice balls and put them in his toilet so he would have water to flush it. I remember hating him with envy because our "rough it" camping allowed everything to be at the mercy of the weather.

Our four horse trailer was sectioned off with one section for food stuffs and cooking supplies, one for tents, and suitcases, one for tack and one for horse food. That hail storm taught us to get better prepared. There were still hail stones left on the ground in the morning.

The second weather story happened at Luzerne Camp on a mostly sunny summer day. Our small group had gone for a ride and had returned to camp. The four horses were tied to picket lines and the feeble fire was smoking our steaks. We watched the clouds thicken up through the leaves of the hardwoods. Some were getting pretty black. It started to thunder and sprinkle, so we grabbed our steaks and ran for the pick-up camper. After only a few bites, the hail started to pound on our roof. The horses were not comfortable and were trying to find a safer spot. We watched the hail pile up on the roof of the horse trailer and decided we had better put the horses inside the trailer. We had just closed the door on the fourth horse when a tree fell across the area where we had been standing loading horses. Then another tree fell across the picket line right where one of the horses had been tied. Other trees and branches fell about the camp. It lasted only about 15 minutes, but it was sure scarey. When it quit, we cleared the brush away from the parking area and went home.

Rex was supposed to be Trail Boss for the 1975 fall ride, but had a major heart attack a week before. Phyllis took over the job, phoning back every day and worrying all day. (He was barely out of the woods when she had to go into it.) He did recover that attack, but died in January of 1976, a great loss to his family and a great loss to the trail rides.

MEMORIES OF MICHIGAN TRAIL RIDING
By Joan Spindler

One of the early memories I have of MTR was a trip in the back of Big Red along the powerline between McKinley Camp and South Branch Camp (Stewart Creek back then). At the bottom of one of those hills, Big Red refused the trip back up. Rex Garn tinkered for a while and finally asked if anyone had a pair of pliers with them. (How many people ride with pliers in their pockets?) Well, someone did and saved the day. The man used to ride with Jack Richards from Livonia. I can't remember the mans name, but he saved the day.

Another time, between South Branch and McKinley, I was driving my truck and trailer across the powerline all by myself. My trailer hitch broke so I left my trailer there and drove back to the Curtisville store. I called trailrider Glenn Hall on the C.B. and explained my problem. Glenn picked me up at the store and drove me to my horse back in camp. I rode the trail to McKinley where I found my rig all repaired and my picket line up. Glen had hauled my trailer into Curtisville. Chuck

Edgecomb had borrowed the use of the welder at Curtisville store and fixed my hitch. Then Chuck picked up a girl with a lame horse and drove my rig into camp.

Another time I lost a wheel off my trailer (the bearings were shot), near Kalkaska Camp. Again, I was rescued by Chuck Edgecomb and Ken Pope. They shopped till they found a bearing that worked to get me across the rest of the ride and home safely.

In the days before the bus, there was Big Red, Glen Hall's van and Bill Zettle's camper. Bill and Glen would pack people in one on top of another till the springs groaned. Many a bottle passed around in Bill's camper. I always appreciated Bill for letting me ride in front. I surely would have had motion sickness in the backend.

I don't know what the story is about dogs always being on a leash, but I remember when they used to be allowed on the trail. My understanding of one of the reasons they are no longer on the trail is because Claude Murdock got bucked off his horse out behind Lost Creek Sky Ranch. He blamed it on a dog. I was riding with him a year later, near the same spot, and his horse again bucked him with no dog in sight.

We call Dottie Vincent the social director as for years she has been calling ahead to let the bars know when the Trail Riders were coming so they would have a band. Dottie loves to dance. Our husbands, Bob and John, used to come along and dance with us, but neither one cares about riding. Now they just show up occasionally. We sure missed the Whispering Pines bar and the camp by Lumberman's Monument for a long time.

You know there are some days you just shouldn't ride. It was a dreary day in October, starting out from Goose Creek to Babbitts. Jato Davis from Owosso, Brad Elrod from Toledo, Lori Falk from St. Clair, and I were on our way. Brads day started out real bad because for some reason he had removed the stirrups from his English saddle and had forgotten to replace them. It's bad enough riding a big saddlebred with no stirrups, but getting on is a real challenge also. As the day progressed the weather turned to freezing rain. Barb and Ken Pope rode by us looking not very happy, so I caught up with them and rode the rest of the way into camp. Our salvation when we arrived dripping and freezing, was Chuck Edgecomb, who had a large camper and a good heater. After tending our horses, we all piled into his camper for cocoa and peppermint schnapps. Ken and Brad took turns playing the guitar and we all sang and laughed about the awful day of riding.

That wasn't the only cold, wet ride I had. You know the trail boss always warns us not to water in certain lakes between Shecks and Kalkaska. Well, it was a rainy day and we were moving right along when we decided to just give our horses a sip at the edge. About that time someone came up right behind me and my horse took that one fatal step forward and I tumbled right over his head as his feet sank into the marl bottom. He swam out turned around and came back, but it was a soggy ride into Kalkaska.

I used to ride quite often with Barb and Ken Pope and Ray Klementi. They had smaller, shorter coupled horses than what I usually rode. Those guys used to love to canter in the woods. It was a real pole bending contest only my horse didn't bend quite as easily as theirs. I'm surprised any of us are still able to use our knees. Another time we were circle riding near Gerry Lake when Ken's horse stepped out too far in a lake and just started swimming. Barb was screaming and we just sat there and watched as Ken's horse swam parallel to the shore for some distance. Finally he turned back toward us. It seemed like he was never going to come back to shore.

I hope someone knows the details of Ray Klementi losing his horse on his way home to Albequrque. I think it was in Wisconsin. I know it was missing at least several weeks, maybe most of the summer. He finally had to drive all the way back from New Mexico to pick it up. Soon after that he started borrowing a horse from me or Ken and Barb.

Jane McGuinn and I had a really great time the first time we rode the new trail from Four Mile to Luzerne. There was no footpath, only blue spots. We were moving right along and whomever lost the trail, the other one became the leader. We had a ball that day changing leaders and jumping the many logs on the trail. As the others came into camp, there was a lot of complaining about how rough it was. We thought it was great.

In the early days, we used to have work bees during the trail rides and on layover days. We did a lot of marking and clearing, but some people complained about working on vacation.

SOLO RIDE ACROSS MICHIGAN
by Pat Schamber, Perrysville, Ohio

My first Michigan crossing on the 240 mile Shore to Shore Riding Hiking Trail was in 1971 on a 13 hand mustang mare, back when the trail went from Elberta to East Tawas and included Lost Creek Sky Ranch. This was a great experience, and I became permanently hooked. In 1974 I was lucky enough to be one of the first six riders to double-cross Michigan. This was so much fun that I looked forward to the next double. But for the next two years circumstances (namely, a new granddaughter and a short illness) limited me to the shorter rides. In 1977, after eagerly planning on another double crossing at last, I learned to my chagrin that only a single crossing was scheduled that year. Being the stubborn type, I determined to make the return ride anyway, by golly, alone except for my grey Arabian mare, Mara.

My husband, Ed, and I rode with the MTRA group on the scheduled crossing, west to east, and at each camp in an out-of-the-way place, we left a half bale of hay in a plastic bag with a note attached to discourage anyone from disturbing it. We also buried bags of grain and salt for the horse and food and extra supplies for me. I drew detailed directions to the caches and also took notes on every tricky turn in the trail to aid my memory.

The end of the scheduled crossing was at East Tawas, and after riding to Lake Huron and then back to the last camp (which in those days was "Trail's End"), Ed drove home to Ohio with his horse and back to work, and I set out alone for South Branch Camp on Mara. That tough little 14 hand mare carried 275 lbs., including her rider, the tack, a pack behind the saddle and the day pack on my back. To save weight, I took a minimum of supplies, mostly basic items such as a tiny backpacking stove, small tent, cooking pot, maps, compass, flashlight, small survival kit, some emergency rations, etc., and a few changes of clothes, but only the one pair of jeans that I was wearing (which was almost my undoing as it turned out!).

The first day and night were rather trying. My little tent slipped out of its place behind the saddle and wasn't missed for some time. I had to backtrack several miles to retrieve it, adding extra length to an already long day's ride. Late that night at South Branch a gang of rough youths from town arrived and on the other side of a patch of trees from me they started a huge bonfire, in spite of dangerously dry conditions, and then proceeded to hold an unmentionable orgy and to use drugs. I cowered in my tent, unable to find my can of mace and afraid to use the flashlight to help locate it, lest it draw their attention. Eventually they left without burning the camp down or seeing me or my mare, but I got no sleep—only a liberal education!

Following the tracks of the first crossing made it easy to find the way for several days, but later on I was temporarily lost a few times — which tends to happen with me!

Approaching McKinley Camp, we were crossing a bog on a plank bridge, when Mara decided it looked better down below and stepped off into deep mire. Somehow she managed to lurch her way out without impaling herself on the snags.

At two camps our buried cache was lost. At Four Mile I just plain couldn't find it and at Kalkaska animals had dug it up. But Mara always had her hay and I had a few granola bars in my day pack, so we never went hungry... On the way to Goose Creek, the zipper broke on my only pair of jeans. My sewing kit came in handy for making an emergency lacing arrangement out of thread, which saved me from a red face... Kind friends came to check on me (my favorite camp cooks even brang sandwiches) at a few of the camps, for which I was grateful, although we were doing just fine! Some new-made friends treated me to a meal and even hot water to wash up in. However I had most camps and the trail entirely to myself.

A few miles from Gary Lake, a big red doe suddenly crashed out of the woods on our right and dashed across the trail almost under Mara's nose. She completely "lost it", and did a 180, heading back for Lake Huron at warp speed. There seemed to be no stopping her. I decided to try a trick that had worked for me before with a runaway. She was wearing her halter over her bridle and I reached up to grab the top of the halter at the poll to pull it down her neck — this gives strong leverage and can even cut off the horse's wind. Unfortunately I goofed and grabbed the top of the bridle instead and pulled it down the neck. (It must have hurt her mouth, poor mare!) She did stop in a hurry and the instant I realized what I had done I quickly pushed the bridle back up again before she could fully react and possibly flip over. Not exactly the method I'd recommend! I'm glad to say she suffered no aftereffects.

We reached Gary Lake Camp (then at the old campsite) on schedule and Ed arrived that evening with the trailer. Next day, minus all the excess baggage, it was a breeze to ride the last short stretch to Empire and Lake Michigan, where we loaded up for home.

The solo ride was worth it all. I had never camped alone before and didn't know if I would be afraid, so it was gratifying to find that I could do it. It was a truly rewarding experience in another way; in those nine and a fraction days, Mara and I were dependent entirely upon each other and we formed a close bond that I still feel as strongly today, even though last year my old friend was buried on our farm.

MORE STORIES:

With the opening of the Shore to Shore Trail, people who normally rode near the cities came to the country. The mixture of city dude and wild country caused some new experiences that were not always fun.

Sally Wilhelm remembers the time they took a group of youngsters out to Jackson Creek from the Rex Ranch. The forest at the top of the hill had been cut and there were brush piles all over. Sally climbed to the top and the kids followed. They no more than got to the top and the horses started to run in all directions. Horses were running and kids were yelling. Finally Sally screamed, "Get off your horses." Sally gave Tony her horse, and he held onto the reins while sitting on Chico. The bees were all over the place. The horses held really still. Sally had the kids lead their horses out of there one by one. None of the kids got stung. Some of the horses must've when they were first running. They could see the bees swarming out of the ground.

Tony tells about the time they were riding over by Empire and for some reason they were off the trail, exploring.. "Bud Weaver was out in front and all of sudden Ben (my horse) stopped still and he was acting like he was marching in place. Everybody behind us was yelling, 'get movin'. But Ben would not move, he just stood in place pounding the ground with his front hooves. I booted him, and I shouldn't have because what he was doing was killing the bees as they were coming out of the ground. When he moved, he got stung and I got stung and everybody else went in different directions. Poor Ben, best horse we ever had."

Tony was asked how long he had Ben. "Not long enough, only 20 years."

I want to tell a couple of bee stories from my experiences. "On one fall ride my oldest daughter and I were riding out of Luzerne on that long, winding trail before you get to the road. We came upon two girls on Appaloosas just moseying along. All of a sudden the one behind started bucking and kicking out his hind feet. The girl must have been inexperienced because she did not try to take up the reins, she just grabbed the saddle horn. He went bucking off through the trees and ran under a low branch, catching the girl by the neck and brushing her off the rear of the horse. He continued to buck until he ran back to his buddy. The girl got up and we asked her if she was all right. She said she was, she guessed. She appeared to be so we rode on. She could've broken her neck.

"Another time on a fall ride, the same daughter and I had just tied up our horses at the top of the bank overlooking Alcona Pond, when a woman on another Appaloosa starting screaming at the same moment her horse started bucking. He pitched her off and ran up the trail a ways. She hit the ground and started to roll and scream. She tore off her jacket, then her shirt and then right down to the skin. She had yellow jackets just clinging to her all over. She just kept rolling and brushing them off with her hands, digging them out from her arm pits and all the other crevices. Finally she stopped. Her friends helped her gather everything up and took care of her. She managed to ride again in a little while and we never did see her after that.

"Another bee incident I witnessed was on the 250 mile race across Michigan. Some people had brought along a small baby and had placed it under the jack pine right across from the pump at Shecks. The baby was young and wrapped up in blankets, placed in one of those plastic bed-chairs people use nowadays. When the riders raced in to the finish line, one of the horses shook some of the branches of the tree. An unseen yellow jacket's nest fell right on the baby and bees coated that poor baby's head and started stinging her. Someone picked up the baby and with their hand scraped the bees off the head. The parents immediately took the baby to emergency. She showed no ill effects from the stings, but the doctor warned the parents that to watch her closely if she got stung in the future, because that was a big load for a small baby."

Tony tells of the time they pulled into Shecks and everybody was crowded down to the other end. He thought, I'll camp down at this end where there is some room. He pulled his rig off to the right and just happened to glance up into a tree. There, right above him, was a big yellow jackets nest with the bees swarming around it. He then knew why everyone had parked at the other end of camp. He said he always looked up in the trees when he was finding a place to park his rig in the fall.

Pat Worden tells of her bee story. " We were circle riding out of Shecks and we were on the south side of the river. We had gone through a bunch of cleared off stuff, there were 7 or 8 of us in that group, and we got into the brush, and all of a sudden here they come. Horses went every which way, and I jumped off, and my horse put his head down and pushed me right out of there. I never got stung, he did. When we got into Shecks his sheath was swelled three times it natural size. I don't remember what vet was in camp, but he gave him some shots and he was fine the next day. It just goes to show you that horses are smarter than people."

Pat Worden, "When you were talking about the girl getting caught under the tree branch reminds me of the time Sally and I had ridden out of Goose Creek. We were coming back from Frederic and it was pouring down rain so we were at a dead run. I had my head right down beside the horse's neck. Sally hollered, 'Look out for the branch', but I didn't know what she hollered. I lifted my head and hollered at her, 'What'd you say?' and wham, that thing hit me and snapped me right on the back of my head. Sally thought I was dead. I was gasping for air and the rain was pouring into my face and mouth. I couldn't talk right for two days."

When they dedicated the trail, the Boy Scouts marched over and Fitch and Tony were leading them on horseback. "Fitch wanted to show me the Morgan property down a little hill thinking the scouts were on foot and he would have time. We were coming back up and Fitch told me to look. I looked and saw the Scouts coming. I remarked to Fitch that I had told him they would march 4 mph. Just about that time, Fitch took off at a canter and my horse did too and a low branch caught me before I could turn around and knocked me off onto the ground. I was lalying there on the ground and Fitch just sat there on his horse laughing."

Sally remembers riding out from her place with Pat Hayes. "There was a fallen tree that a person could get under if they ducked, but I always went around it and I had a little pathway made. It was on a hill going down through a woods. Pat had a little Morgan and I don't think it was really well trained. Anyway, I just loped around it and Pat's horse went under it catching her right in the top of the chest, knocking her back and off her horse and she landed flatter than a pancake. I felt really bad seeing her lay there. She got up and was all right but for some sore places.

That reminded me of a similar thing that happen on the Shore to Shore ride just out of South Branch. A man named Norm Cooper, in his late 50's, was running his horse along that path on the ridge that every once in a while goes both ways around a tree. He thought about going one way, but his horse went the other, and scraped him off under a branch. His horse came tearing into camp without a rider. Some of us ran back down the trail to find Norm. We found him walking toward camp holding his arm at the elbow. We took him into Oscoda and the xray's showed a broken wrist. He was from Wisconsin, so he loaded up on pain pills and stayed the rest of the ride. He said he wanted to make sure who ever fixed it would do a good job and he wanted to check the doctor's expertise that was in Oscoda, because he only wanted to fix it once. That was the end of his endurance racing for that summer. We did see him a few years later and he said his wrist felt fine, that he had had a good surgeon fix it.

Pat Worden tells of the time she was riding with Tony's son with his pony.

"Chris (age 10) always liked to push down dead trees as he rode along. He got me to ride along with him and he pushed one over and it didn't go all the way down. I rode up to it and let myself ride right into it, thinking it would fall on down. It didn't and I was wiped right off my horse. Chris thought that was pretty funny."

Bogs...

Sally tells of the time Jane McGuinn said she knew a short cut to the Manistee Pie Shop. She, Rex, and Tony started to follow her through the woods. It kept getting wetter and wetter. They came to a little creek and Jane said they must be through the worst of it. Sally looked across the creek and there was nothing but black muck and logs. She announced that she was turning around and heading back. There are two things you don't do when you ride with Jane: You never turn around and go back, and you never get off your horse. Sally turned back alone and had ridden quite a while when along came Tony and in a few more minutes, along came Rex. "Later there came Jane, just breezing right past us and madder than a wet hen because we wouldn't go with her. When we went to southern Illinois, we realized why she thought she could go anywhere. Down there, there is always a hard bottom. She didn't realize she could sink out of sight up here in Northern Michigan."

Pat tells about a new trail that Don Abbott had made on the east side of the state. "Sally and I were going to go with him to check it out. When we got to the end of the dirt road, the trail went into the most ungodly swamp you ever saw in your life. When we stepped into it our horses were wading in water. We told him we were not going to take his trail through there. He said 'Any horse can go through there, if it's too wet they can swim, otherwise they can walk on the roots and get through, my stallion can.' We just looked at him, I mean, and he was dead serious. We didn't believe him and went back."

Tony's bog story... "On the first trail ride across the state, we rode up to Pearl Lake when we were camping at Jim Hardy's. Jim went down to get his horse a drink. The ground just shook a little bit and then whoosh, he was gone. All four legs were stuck up to the belly. There were a couple of kids with 2 and 3 year old quarter horses with us. One with a lariat. I got down and dug a tunnel under the horse. It was a nice little stallion and he never struggled, just stood there. We got his saddle off and I reached under and got the lariat under him. Those little quarter horses just snugged him right out of there."

Chris Wilhelm's pony ,Blackie, got away from him at Little Guernsey Lake and floundered around really bad getting black muck over everyone. He eventually managed to get out. The lakes in Michigan have a white clay bottom called marl. They are very tricky.

Bud and Barb tell about a friend of theirs named Paul. They were coming from Kalkaska and were just about to the Guernsey Lakes. Bud told Paul not to drink at the lake on the left, but to go down to the next lake on the right, it's solid and everything. "Barb and I got a drink of lemonade from another friend and got back on our horses. I went over the rise by Little Guernsey Lake and there was Paul down there in that drink. I looked at Barb, and she said, "I don't believe it." I said, "I do." He was riding an old roan walkin' horse and Norma was riding that big old bay quarter horse of his. I walked down, and this old horse wouldn't hold his head out of the water. Paul had to stand there and hold his head up so he wouldn't drown. Finally I went back and got our tie ropes and backed that old quarter horse back up in there. We got the tie rope on the halter of Paul's horse and I got a half hitch on the saddle horn and Norma lead that big old quarter horse until I couldn't hold him. Finally we got the quarter horse backed up a little bit further and I got a good hold on that saddle horn. When that old quarter horse felt that rope tighten up, he just gave a big hunch and tipped that roan horse right out of there. Just tipped him right over and dragged him out of there. I told Paul to get on down to the lake on the right where he was supposed to water. Dang, I was mad at him. When you take the time to warn somebody about a danger and they ignore it, then you have to rescue them, it makes me angry."

The bogs and lakes of Michigan could probably tell a lot of stories. Back in the summer of 1970, Roger, myself, and my two daughters were riding on a trail ride out of Gordon Creek Camp. One of the young men took a short cut through a swamp and mired his horse up in some mud. His horse fought it's way out, but wrenched it's back in the process. He was trailered back to camp where he went into shock and died. That lesson taught us to be very careful about crossing Michigan mud.

Joanne Spindler ~ Kathy Helsig ~ Jane McManus

126

THE PEOPLE
Ch. 13

Certificate of Recognition

In Recognition of those Individuals who Gave Generously
of their Time and Physical Effort to the
Creation and Development of the
Michigan Shore to Shore
Riding & Hiking Trail.

May All Those who Ride or Walk the trail Remember these
Individuals Without Whose Efforts This Trail
Would Not Exist.

The Michigan Riding and Hiking Trail brought people together under a common bond: the horse. The friendships that have been formed by the simple act of attending a trail ride were not even in the image of the success of having a trail that could be ridden across the state. In the beginning the emphasis was on just getting from shore to shore on a horse.

When Sally and Tony Wilhelm visited Jim Hardy and the subject of riding their horses from Lake Michigan to Lake Huron came into the conversation, they knew it was just something they'd like to do. That was the beginning of many lasting friendships.

When people arrived at the beginning of the trail rides they were strangers, but by the time they lived together in the woods for 10 days, they were friends. The very first ride across in 1964 brought together the Wilhelms, the Williams, the Garns, Jim Hardy, Harold Pence, Jane McGuinn, the Broegmans, the Lannens, and the Heims. This small nucleus was a driving force to the future success of the trail.

Many of the people who joined had special things they could offer. Bud Weaver had a camper factory, he could design and make a chuck wagon to make it easier for the cooks to prepare the food. Other people like Glen Hall (An ex-railroad worker who liked to make all the trails follow abandoned railroad beds.), Bill Zettle (Who has made at least 40 crossings.), Bill

Babbitt, (Always happy to have riders stay at his ranch to and from Elk Hill.), all became useful for taking care of a section of the trail. Another, like Fred Stackable, an attorney, who lived down state and could mediate with the state officials. Fred rewrote the by-laws for the organization. Certain men of the Forest Service and State Conservation Department became good friends and some even witnessed the trail from the back of someones horse. Roger Moore, Dennis Vitton, Fred Haskins, Forest Rhodes, (who almost went over Alcona pond and then bought the horse.) This experience first hand led to a lot of insight as to the problems.

Some loaned equipment and others had only their time. Most drove long distances to help when work bees needed attendance. Whatever they had to offer was greatly appreciated. Gwen Grinager took on the job of historian. Joe and Leona Reicha cooked many a meal in the rain and the snow.

People like Bob Barlow, Gwen Grinager, rode until they could ride no more.

Some people came every year and brought their families and friends. Then they would go home and get ready for next year. Then there was a fellow we all called Gramps who didn't ride it, but he brought all his grandchildren year after year. Andy Yeip (board member) and Roy Williams, from Port Huron, came to many work bees. They always wore Carhartt jackets and were nicknamed Mr. Car & Mr. Hartt. Jack Van Dyke and Royce Wilson, from Sparta came up to many work bees. A group from St. Johns who came to many work bees and were probably the first to pack and ride across the state with horses only, were Earl Andrus, Albert Schultz, Clyde Manville, Fred Strouse, Vern Kowalk, and Clinton Smith.

The group from the Mio area were very instrumental in creating the trail: Marily Blomfield, Jim Hardy's right hand wrangler; Forrest Rhodes was with the United States Forest Service when he helped Jim lay out the original trail on the east side of the state; Ray Clementi, a very nice man was from that area also. There was a group called the Bad Axe crew: Mary and Don McIntyre (board member) and attended work bees; Larry and Sharon Day-Carpenter, both helped in their own way. Larry played guitar at campfires and Sharon was trail boss quite a few times. Her nickname was "Shady Day". Also from Bad Axe was Clayton Day, Cindy Smith, Charlene Ignach, and Artie Smith.

Joanne Spindler, long time member and attended many work bees. Jim and Pat Hayes, (board member) and attended work bees. Virginia and Bernell Franklin and children. Virginia, (board member) and past President, was always on work bees, laid out new trails, located new camps, etc. In the late 80's Virginia Franklin created another trail riding group that rides the trail, shore to shore, every June. She limits it to no more than 100 riders so that she can keep track of everybody and make sure they get there all right. Terry Lautner, (board

128

member) and past President plus attended work bees. Dottie Vincent, long time member and attended many work bees. Les Botimer, (board member) and worked on bees. Duane "Bud" Weert, donated art work for guidebook. Les Biederman, owner of Midwestern Broadcasting Co., contributed the printing of the first buidebook. Don Abbott, (board member) provided hay on the east side of the state.

George and Alita Stump, (board member) past President, and attended work bees. Jim Schriber owned Trails End Ranch outside Tawas where the trail riders camped after the closing of Gordon Creek. Joyce Frank (board member) and nice lady. Lois Godfrey came to many work bees. Bill and Ginger Vanderkallen, (both were board members) and attended work bees. Malcom and Betty Young, put on horseback games at Goose Creek Camp for the kids. Bill Gillette, owned a bar and always brought a bushel of Peaches & Cream wine. Dallas Harvey, rode his horse into Friendly Tavern in Empire and they gave his horse a beer. Carl Seaver from Zilwaukee, played his guitar at campfires. Harry DeHaan, arrived at Empire once with his horse upside down laying on his back in the trailer, next morning he left with pots, pans and coffee pot hanging from his saddle. We nicknamed him "Klank" and said he was an accident looking for a place to happen. Forrest Hall, Glen's dad helped on work bees. Russell "Bud" Weaver (board member) past President, came to many work bees, donated the chuckwagon to MTRA.

Ted McManus, helped Bud Weaver haul oak lumber into Mayhem Swamp for new bridges, with the aid of Kate the mulc. Also, loaned his tractor and loader to Bud for filling of mud holes with gravel at Sheck's Camp. Dick Penfold, long time member and rider. Ray Purvis and David Crouch helped on many work bees. Keith Seaman, long time member, came to work bees, and drove the big red stock truck for shuttle for a time. Don and Marge Radtke from North Street, came to many work bees. Jim and Faith Aseltine, good supporters of the trail. Judy Schlink (board member), helped anywhere she could. She'd help Glen Hall, Harold Babbitt, and Doc Lannen mark trail whenever she could get away from work. She lost her beautiful Arab gelding to Swamp Fever after going on the June ride one spring. After her loss, they decided to ask for a Coggins test from horses out of state. You'll also see her name in the endurance section.

I do want to give a special tribute to Bob Broegman who has stayed with the organization since 1964. This year was his 18th year for being trail boss, which means six rides a year now. Right beside his side is Evelyn. They have witnessed a lot of changes in the trail and the people, but they have faith that whatever problems arrive the trail ride will go on, from shore to shore, across the state of Michigan.

There is another person who deserves special credit here and anyone I talked to could only say good things about her. Her name is Jane McGuinn and she lives near Chicago, IL. She is mentioned here and there throughout the book, but really deserved a whole chapter written about her. Pat Worden says that she was better known as "Mother McGuinn".

Following are some experiences Pat wanted to share with us about Jane: "I don't remember the year, but I sure remember my first encounter with Jane. We were riding from Empire. My mare had foaled early in the year and I had just weaned the foal. By the time we got to Gerry Lake Camp her bag was swollen and was as hard as a rock. Rex came over to help me relieve her from some of her milk. Jane arrived just about then and said "I've got just the stuff to dry her up fast" and rubbed this white liniment on her bag, then stepped back quick as the crowd started to gather around. Within minutes my poor old mare was jumping, bucking, and carrying on something awful. I was yelling not very nice things at Jane. Finally I got my mare settled down, but I wasn't. I loaded her in the trailer and took her home. The next day Rex and Jane came over to my house to make amends. Rex was still laughing, however Jane wasn't. She asked me to come back on the ride. I did, and from that day on Jane and I spent many wonderful hours, weeks, years riding together.

"Jane liked to spend as much time off the trail exploring as she did riding on the trail. Jane's short cuts sometimes ended up being miles out of the way, but she still arrived at the next camp before most riders and always had wonderful tales to tell about the days ride. Jane's rig was almost like a sporting goods store. She always had lots of games for old and young alike. As I recall, it was Jane who started laundromat volleyball games in Kalkaska. Sure made doing trail laundry more fun; even the men offered to do laundry.

"One year she brought Christmas stuff along and that started the Christmas caroling night at Goose Creek Camp. At first not everyone was ready for those kinds of antics, but it wasn't long before most joined the fun. Jane is a very learned person when she talks about countries and other things she's been to and seen. You feel like you've been there and seen it too.

"I don't know a better horsewoman or a more gracious lady. She made a difference in my life and for many others who know her."

There are probably many people who helped along the way that I have not heard about. There are probably enough to write another book about. I mainly wanted to write this book about the people whose ideas made the whole thing possible and tell about the beginning. I remember meeting a lot of the people listed above and there are special reasons why I have not forgotten them. But, those are the kind of personal things that are nice to remember, but boring to write about.

Approximate Distances Via Trail Between Prominent Points

	Miles
Empire to Gerry Lake Trail Camp (State Forest)	9
Golden Valley Ranch to Gerry Lake	9
Gerry Lake to Mud Lake Trail Camp (S.F.)	16
Elberta to Wallin Trail Camp (S.F.)	21
Bakers Acres to Wallin	4
Wallin to Mud Lake Trail Camp (S.F.)	12
Mud Lake to Scheck's Trail Camp (S.F.)	25
Spring Valley Ranch & Rex Ranch to Scheck's	13
Scheck's to Hopkins Creek Trail Camp (S.F.)	20
Hopkins Creek to Gateway Trail Camp (S.F.)	20
Scheck's to Kalkaska Trail Camp (S.F.)	20
Ranch Rudolph to Kalkaska	19
Kalkaska to Goose Creek Trail Camp (S.F.)	27
Sky Valley Ranch to Goose Creek	20
Goose Creek to Grayling	13
Babbitt's Riding Stable to Grayling	12
Grayling to 4-Mile Trail Camp (S.F.)	7
4 Mile to McKinley T.C. (Trail Riders Assn.)	40
Lost Creek Sky Ranch to McKinley	17
McKinley to Stewart Creek T.C. (Trail Riders Assn.)	18
Stewart Creek to Gordon Creek (National Forest)	13
Gordon Creek to Tawas City (Community)	15
Tawas Trail Riders Corral to Tawas City	3
Grayling to Elk Hill Trail Camp (State Forest)	55

Approximate distance via trail from Elberta and Empire on Lake Michigan to Tawas City on Lake Huron—210 miles.

PART TWO

Individual maps of the trail
from camp to camp
with changes from 1963 - 1995

EMPIRE
TO
MUD LAKE

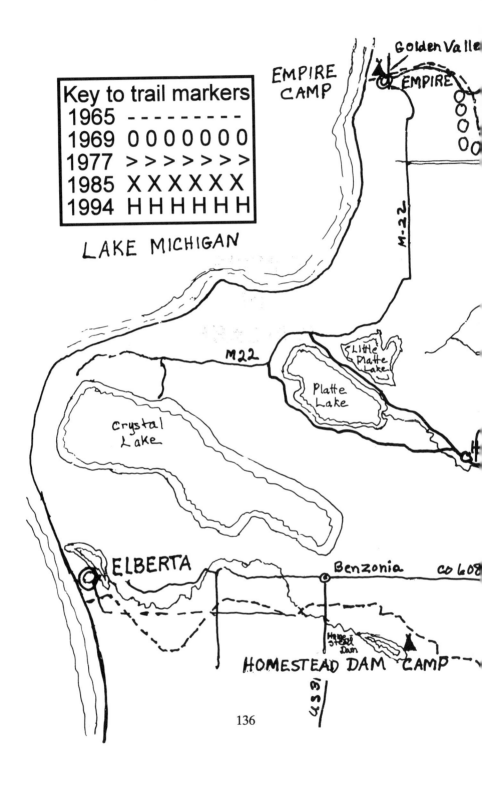

Key to trail markers
1965 - - - - - - - - -
1969 0 0 0 0 0 0 0
1977 > > > > > > >
1985 X X X X X X
1994 H H H H H H

LAKE MICHIGAN

Golden Valle

EMPIRE CAMP

EMPIRE

M-22

M22

Little Platte Lake

Platte Lake

Crystal Lake

ELBERTA

Benzonia

Co 608

HOMESTEAD DAM CAMP

Homestead Dam

439

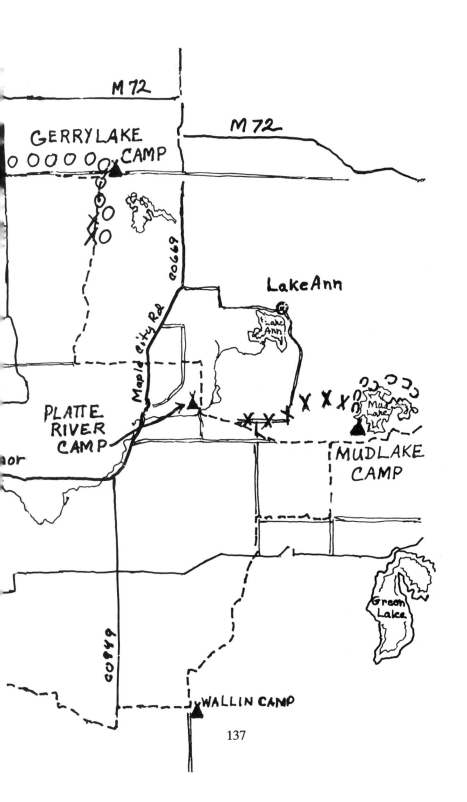

M 72

M 72

GERRYLAKE CAMP

o o o o o o

Maple City Rd

CO 669

LakeAnn

Lake Ann

PLATTE RIVER CAMP

X X X X

Mud Lake

MUDLAKE CAMP

nor

CO 949

Green Lake

WALLIN CAMP

137

EMPIRE TO MUD LAKE

The Michigan Riding and Hiking Trail follows the highway (M-72) east out of empire for about 4 miles. Then it turns south onto an old railroad bed lined with pines. It is a pretty unique railroad bed because if you stop to think of all the dirt that had to be moved to make it, you marvel at the optimism of whoever had the idea it could be done.

From M-72 it is about 9 miles to Gerry Lake Camp. The trail is two track and sandy and the trees are mostly pine.

Gerry Lake Camp is on top of a hill overlooking Gerry Lake. It used to be at the bottom of the hill beside the lake. The lake is safe for horses to enter and has a good bottom for horse bathing. the campground is peaceful and sometimes you can hear loons calling at night. There is a good hand pump at the lower camp. On top of the hill is a pump that can be hooked to a motor home generator.

To get to Gerry Lake Campground by car, take M-72 west almost to Empire. On a curve to the right will be a road going left (Co. Rd. 669). Follow 669 a few miles to Pittingill Rd., turn right onto it, and go quite a few miles. Camp is on the left.

The trail from Gerry Lake to Mud Lake is approximately 18 miles in length. It immediately goes into the woods. First hardwoods, then open places and then back to hardwoods for about 9 miles before you see a blacktop road. There are also some lakes that are beautiful in the fall with the colored leaves reflecting in them.

The blacktop road is Co. Rd. 669. You cross that and ride another two-track, this one called Hooker Rd. About a mile on this, again beautiful hardwoods, and you will come to a dirt road.

This is a nice smooth dirt road (not gravel) that you can move right along on. Just a couple of houses along it. When you get to a corner, you will be on a gravel road and it will wind around a hill and down to the culvert that crosses the Platte River. It is a beautiful river, but there isn't anyplace to water your horse.

Up the hill to the left and enter beautiful hardwoods again. About a half mile and you come to a creek crossing under the road. Here, at the left, you can water your horse.

About another half mile and you will come to a gravel road. A few lucky people live along here. A half mile of gravel and you find a paved road to cross(Reynold's Rd.)

Cross Reynolds Rd and you are now on Bronson Rd. This is gravel and more lucky people live along here. This road brings you to pavement that you have to turn left onto to get you back across the Platte River before you can turn right onto Douglas Lake Rd. This turns into a two-track and from here it is about 2 1/2 miles until you get to Mud Lake Camp. The woods is the usual mixture of Michigan trees with quite a bit of Popple in one part of it. Makes me wonder when the beaver will find it.

Even though there is some gravel road riding, this is a beautiful trail if you like woods and woodland creatures. Quite a variety of birds live here and their songs are better than any man made music. A baby porcupine stands in the road and seems quite unafraid. All sorts of spring flowers that you will see only in hardwoods.

The Mud Lake Camp ground is one of the most beautiful of all the camps. The flooding makes a good sized lake (now called Lake Dubbonet) and the hardwoods make nice shade, yet it seems so open and cool. There is a place you can water your horse at the edge of the lake. Won't swear about how good the bottom is farther out. The pump is good and there are pit toilets.

If you wanted to take your horse there in a trailer, you would go out U.S. 31 past the golf course to Gonder Rd. Take a right and go about a mile. You will come to Mud Lake Rd. where you will take a left. Follow that a little ways until you come to Lake Dubbonet Rd. where you will turn right and go about a mile until you cross a dam with a creek on your left and a lake on your right. Right across this dam, on your right is Mud Lake Campground. The camp ground follows the lake quite a distance. You will see the Blue Trail off to your left as you turn into camp. At the other end of the camp ground the Blue Trail that goes on to the next camp continues on around the lake heading east.

Even if you do not want to ride to Gerry Lake, this is a wonderful area to just circle ride because there are many trails that leave this camp.

Go get your horse and go for it. You fed the bugger all winter!

MUD LAKE
TO
SHECKS

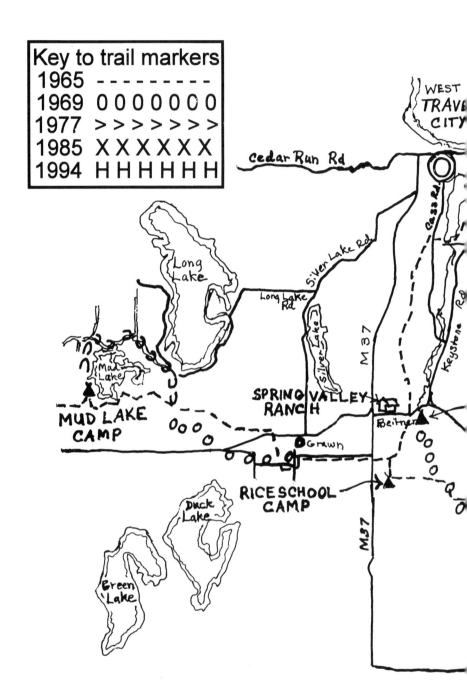

Key to trail markers
1965 - - - - - - - - - -
1969 O O O O O O O
1977 > > > > > > >
1985 X X X X X X
1994 H H H H H H

WEST
TRAVE
CITY

Cedar Run Rd

Cass Rd

Silver Lake Rd

Long Lake

Long Lake Rd

Keystone Rd

M 37

Silver Lake

SPRING VALLEY
RANCH

Beitner

Mud Lake

MUD LAKE
CAMP

O O O O O

Grawn

RICE SCHOOL
CAMP

Duck Lake

M 37

Green Lake

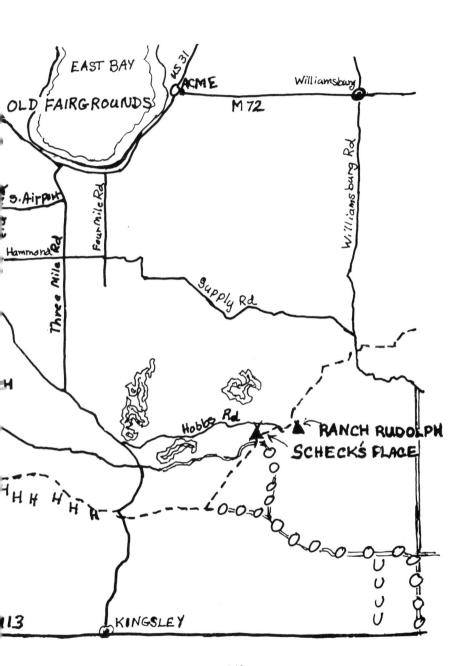

MUD LAKE TO SHECKS
ON A HOT DAY IN AUGUST

The temperature is 92 degrees in the shade. As I sit in front of my computer battling this heat, it takes me back to the time I rode alone from Mud Lake to Shecks.

I was trying to get my horse in condition for the 250 mile race across Michigan. It consisted of five days of fifty mile distances each day. I remember it was early August and I wanted a good strenuous two day work out to help prepare my horse for the competition three weeks away.

I parked my camper at the Mud Lake Campground Saturday morning and rode toward Empire, and then back to the rig. The weather was not too bad for riding, only in the mid eighties.

By midnight Saturday night, when it hadn't cooled down, I knew Sunday was going to be brutal. I planned to leave by 7 a.m..,but didn't leave until 8. I packed 24 ounces of water for me and electrolytes for the horse.

I started east out of Mud Lake, feeling tired because I hadn't slept well in the heat. The trail around the lake was especially beautiful in the morning. The woods are mostly hardwoods so you have a good cover from the sun, and it's open enough to allow grass to grow here and there. I spied a baby fawn standing very still. Something else must have startled it because he held perfectly still in a frozen state, hoping I wouldn't see him. My horse, a spooky beast, saw it. In an instant we landed on the other side of the rode, and my back muscles told me they felt that one.

The hard-packed sand road was perfect for trotting. When we arrived at Long Lake Rd. there was a nice creek. The bank was firm and I decided to offer my horse a drink. I put him down the bank into the water, but he wouldn't drink. My old veteran trail horse usually tanked up every chance he had, but this new Arab thinks his trailer is just around the corner.

We crossed Long Lake Rd. This was a bad place to cross with four steel shoes and a slightly slanted, paved road, on a corner of a busy highway. We made it without slipping, and onto some more nice sand footing. I took up the trot again, and watched for blue dots carefully, because this part is like a maze.

Finally, we came to That Garn Bridge. I helped build this 40 foot long bridge. It was named in memory of Rex Garn who was the chairman of the committee to build a bridge across the end of Ellis Lake. He died before he could build it.

After the bridge is just a little bit of woods before a gravel road bringsthe trail out onto U.S.31 S. The trail crosses the busy highway at this point, because it is the best sight distance for traffic. It turns left and follows the road just a little ways and then branches off onto the road through Grawn. I knew I had four miles of riding next to this pavement, across people's lawns, driveways, barking dogs, kids playing, people on bikes, and cars. We trotted whenever there weren't any of the

145

aforementioned obstacles. It was hot. I had finished one of my containers of water by the time I got to M-37.

Crossing M-37 is not easy either, although you can see traffic for a long ways. It is very slippery for shod horses. I guess I wouldn't have worried so much if my horse weren't so inclined to come unglued.

More paved road and more houses, but for only, maybe, a mile. Finally, the back of the fairgrounds and I turned onto the two-track east towards the woods. It was about 11 a.m. and the sun had done a number on me going through Grawn. I tapped into my other container of water. A couple of swallows—I felt better. Let's try the trot.

That shady stretch was too short and I found myself out in the sun again. The breeze was hot coming off the parched open areas. I drank some more. Some trees greeted me up ahead. I felt light headed and really tired. I thought I'd walk a ways. My horse didn't mind hanging his head and walking my speed, he must have felt the heat also. I finished my drink and got back on. I thought Jackson Creek was just around the corner and I could make it. Maybe the next corner. I hadn't remembered so many corners before. Yes, I was on the right trail because one of those DNR signs of the hoof and horse shoe was visible on a tree to the left. Up ahead I saw it; the turn to the left that would take me down the big hill to Jackson Creek.

That rippling creek, hidden at the bottom seemed to be made just for me. The horse drank this time. I jumped in with my high-top tennis shoes and splashed water on my face and neck. I thought I would live. I tied up the horse and unsaddled him. Off came the tee shirt which was thrown into the creek. I washed everything above the waist and below the knees. I drank more water. I knew I could get Giardia, but at this point I wouldn't make it home if I didn't drink. I dunked my head and put the wet tee shirt back on. Whoa! That was cold on my hot body.

I then bathed the horse with his sponge. He acted like it felt good. Time came to leave. I re-saddled, electrolyted the horse with a cut-off 20 cc syringe. (My electrolyte mixture consists of Morton's Lite Salt, calcium carbonate and magnesium.) I put a little on my wet finger and dabbed it on my tongue. A little grainy, but not too bad. I took a little more, rinsed my mouth with Jackson Creek water, filled up my two containers and mounted up.

I felt like a new person as we climbed the steep hill out of the creek bed. Large maple trees shaded us so we trotted.

Soon we entered oil country. Civilization again with gravel roads and oil wells. Another place to watch for the signs carefully, because getting through here is tricky. A deer jumped up and snorted in the bushes. My horse shied and tried to bolt. We both must have had full control of our bodies to handle that, so I felt I might make it.

It's just a couple of miles to the Mayfield Store (the burg itself is not noteworthy, but that store has saved more than a few lives). We came out of the

146

woods and onto a gravel road. Down a curved hill, over the dam, ah horse, I said over the dam. Finally, thank you, now we can get on to the store.

After I ate the ice cream cone, I packed a can of coke into my bags, mounted and rode on, drinking an ice cold Coco Cola. Along the paved road a little ways further on, the trail turned into the woods. Nice hardwoods. Nice and cool. A mile later and we reached a stream. My horse drinks again. Electrolyte time again. A little more wouldn't hurt me either. We should make Shecks about 3 p.m..

We were both refreshed and the road was sandy so we cantered up a long hill, along a level area. Oops! Almost missed the turn off to the left. Nice cool woods would be ahead of me all the way to the river. The road crosses the river on a bridge so there isn't any place to water, but no matter, we would be at Shecks in a few minutes. The trail goes past the people camp, through some pines, then some aspen, and when you enter the open field, you are at Shecks Place Campground. A camper here and there, but we didn't have time to visit, we went straight to the river. The horse drank again. The Boardman river at this point, is deep enough to swim a horse. It's best to do this bareback and save your saddle. I drank at the pump and filled my containers again. The best water in the world comes out of these camp pumps!

I couldn't dilly-dally today, I had twelve more miles to go before I would get home. Out on the road someone driving by stopped when they saw me off my horse fixing something on the saddle that was slipping. I was not dressed in the usual cowboy garb, so they asked me why I was wearing tennis shoes, leg leathers, and a helmet. I told them I was an endurance rider. They ask me if I knew Rhoda Ritter? They were interested in learning more about the sport and was told to find Rhoda. They were told that they'd have to look in the woods, not at her house.

I laughed and told them they had found her.

That made my day. For all of the suffering of the heat out there in the woods, at least someone had heard of me.

Two more cokes at Ranch Rudolf and I headed home. I was about four hours behind schedule but I made it. I remember that day. My horse worked well for me and I began to really like him.

Elk at Elk Hill

Elk Hill Camp - Norm Draper

SHECKS
TO
KALKASKA

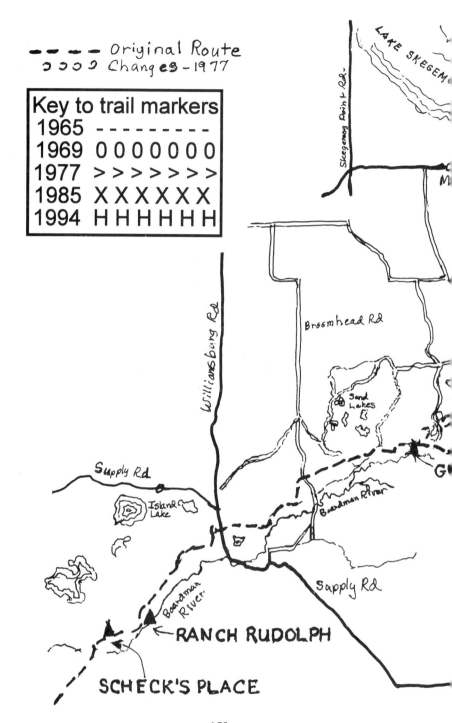

Original Route

ɔ ɔ ɔ ɔ ɔ Changes - 1977

Key to trail markers
1965 - - - - - - - - -
1969 0 0 0 0 0 0 0
1977 > > > > > > >
1985 X X X X X X
1994 H H H H H H

LAKE SKEGEM

Skegemog Point Rd.

M

Broomhead Rd

Williamsburg Rd

Sand Lakes

G

Supply Rd

Island Lake

Boardman River

Boardman River

Supply Rd

←RANCH RUDOLPH

SCHECK'S PLACE

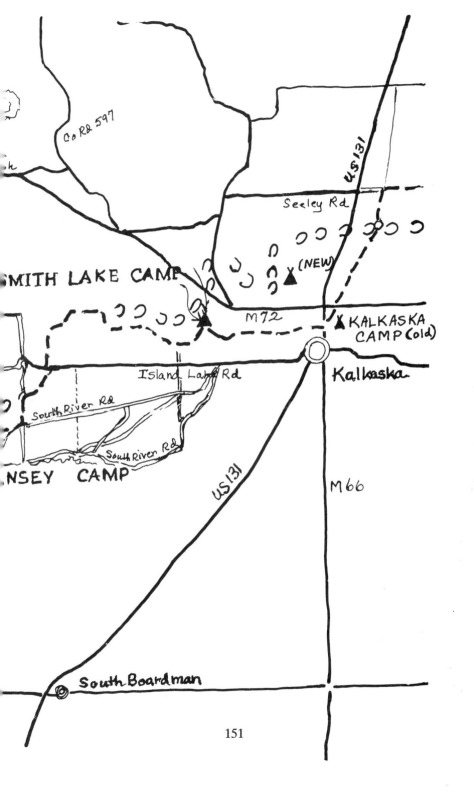

Co Rd 597

US 131

Seeley Rd

SMITH LAKE CAMP

(NEW)

M 72

KALKASKA
CAMP (old)

Island Lake Rd

Kalkaska

South River Rd

South River Rd

NSEY CAMP

US 131

M 66

South Boardman

SHECKS TO KALKASKA

The Michigan Riding and Hiking Trail, from Shecks to Kalkaska is all single pathway through the woods. I rode it alone one sunday in July when the weather was perfect for riding a horse. It left me feeling very much at peace and also thankful that we have such a wonderful trail to ride.

Shecks Campground is found by car by taking the Brown Bridge Road off from Supply Road just as Supply crosses the Boardman River. Follow Brown Bridge Road for six miles, passing Ranch Rudolf as you cross the river again, and continue until you see the Trail Camp sign on your right. You turn left down a two-track for about half a mile until you come to a big open area. There will be a big sign and plenty of places to park your rig. The Boardman River is just to the left (south) of the campground.

To get out of Shecks Campground there is a path at the northest corner of the camp, just past the sign. It will take you out to the road, which you cross, and follow the side of the road until you cross the gravel road at the bottom of a big hill. It then turns left and climbs a steep hill. At the top is a two-track which you will cross and follow the blue dots down a single path. As you ride along, you will see many trails and many blue dots. These are trails for riding, hiking, and skiing from Ranch Rudolf. There should be a capital H on a tree every once in a while to signify the horse trail. If you have a compass, bare in mind, you are heading east.

There are also many two track roads through here that you will either ride down or cross; just follow the blue dots or the DNR plastic signs that are blue with the white horse shoe print and human shoe print. the trees are tall oaks and maples, with a beech here and there. You can see a long ways and sometimes catch a glimpse of a white tail deer trying to escape you. About four miles of this and you will cross Supply Road. The trail used to cross on the hill via the two-track, but it was moved to the crest of the hill for safety reasons. The pathway that takes you through the woods is solid ground, whereas, if you took the two-track, it would be very sandy. They meet at the banks of the Boardman River. Watering used to be allowed here, although by the time your horse climbed back up the sandy bank, the horse was probably thirsty again, but now there has been a renovation of the river and you should not ruin the work of many people by trying to get to the water.

This "used to be" watering spot is a memorable spot for me, because I got dumped off my horse in the big hole in the middle of the main flow. She had hit some wire across the trail about two hours back and from then on was skittish about every stick she saw across the trail. When she was belly deep in the river drinking, I dropped my sponge and let it flow down stream to soak up water. As I pulled it back toward her, as I had done at 5000 times before this, she caught this thing coming toward her and spun in a 360 degree circle. I only made it 180 of the degrees and landed in the water. When I came up, I saw my girl friend just as she grabbed my

153

horse at the top of the hill. Her horse had luckily taken off with mine and she managed to reach out and grab her. My mare would have run the 12 miles to our ranch. A year later I rode the same horse into the same spot and she was very wary, looking for whatever got her last time.

The trail follows this two-track for a way along the river. When there isn't a lot of foliage, you can see the river many times as you ride this ridge. Watch for the left turn that pulls you off and onto a single path again. This brings you out at a big oil storage station on Broomhead Road.

On the other side of the road you enter the Quiet Area. A little more open and bushy, also more pines. The Quiet Area is a place set aside for peace and quiet; no motorized vehicles are allowed in there, winter or summer. There are trails marked with blue dots and DNR signs with backpackers and skiers on them. The horse trail goes straight east and is marked with the usual sign, plus at the crossroads are 4x4 posts with the official blue top and the horse shoe-human foot print carved into them with directing arrows.

You will come to a fork in the path, going up a small hill. If you go to the right, you will arrive at the old halfway campground on the boardman River. It used to be a good place to water a horse, but the water is high this year and the big tree has been washed out, so the entrance to the river is muddy and the water swift. No matter, just around the corner is Guernsey Lake and that has a perfect place to water.

To find your way out of this campground, you will follow the faintly marked trail just to the left of the entrance road. This connects to the trail back down the hill that you left when you made the right turn to the river. This is a bit confusing, but bare in mind again that you are going east and when you come to this trail, go right.

At Guernsey Lake there is a deep gully that leads to the lake. the lake bottom is very solid and we are allowed to water our horses there. Further along this trail there is another lake to the right. The bottom to this lake is very soft and you never try to enter there. Horses have gotten mired down over the saddle horns in there. In fact, do not water in any lake in Michigan unless you are very sure of the bottom. Michigan lakes have a white clay that allows a horse to sink in to the point where he will need help getting out. That white clay is called marl.

At the gravel road, past the bad lake, the trail goes right only a little ways and then turns left into the woods again. There are some new signs fastened to the posts. They say "National Scenic Pathway". I'm not sure what they mean, because this is state land, not national.

A nice single pathway, turning some 90 degree corners and exposed root systems is up ahead. A new dirt road has been put through here. This was a puzzleing spot because I could not see a marker telling me to turn, nor did I see one telling me to go straight. The old trail used to go straight, so I went straight. It was at least 3/4 of a mile before I saw my reassuring DNR marker, and then I saw three very close together. I almost took one off to take back and put on the corner, but I thought I'd better not tamper with this trail. Probably the reason it was messed up was the fault of someone else's tampering.

Again, the trail crosses a dirt road and enters a single pathway through some high pines. A good place to canter, so canter I did. Way ahead I saw a fawn jump up and go leaping through the pines, out of my sight. My horse saw it too and came to a screeching halt.

When I came to the end of the pines and crossed the two-track to go down a steep hill into some more pines, I saw it was very eroded. A big tree root was across it waiting to trap my horse's leg and snap it. I decided not to go down beside it because the hill was covered with slippery pine needles and my horse wears shoes on his hind feet. I turned right on the two-track and rode just a short ways and I found a trail going left into the woods. Just a few steps and I came to the corner of the blue trail.

As I rode along, I couldn't make up my mind whether to soak up the view of Island Lake and it's shoreline on my left, or keep my eyes on the forest with it's mingling of white birch and sun beams. Why does a sunbeam seem so magic as it comes down through the leaves of a birch and strikes the ground or the white bark of the tree?

I managed to get myself out of my dreamy state and cross Island Lake Road. Now the trees were maples, oaks, and beeches; much darker and cooler. It was fun through here, trotting until I came to a log across the path or a small eroded hill. I passed an old tree stump that was hit by lightning at least ten years ago; not much left of her. It is so quiet and peaceful, I must be in the middle of nowhere.

Finally the trail comes out at some oil storage tanks and a gravel road. Just a little ways down the road and it turns back into the woods on a single path again and more peace. (It was in this particular oil well area that my mare hit the wire that caused me to get dumped in the river.)

I arrived at Glen Hall's favorite trail; the railroad bed. But wait, something has changed. The rows and rows of red pines have been cut and the ones that are left are scattered randomly throughout the forest. They look really nice. There isn't any brush left over from the harvest and I want to thank whoever did the job. There is still the sand in part of the railroad bed that I could have done without, but it had just rained the day before so it was not dusty. By now I am getting sick of the cob webs across my glasses and mouth. Some of them are pretty strong. The ferns are everywhere and they hide the trail until you turn every corner to find it.

Eventually we reach M-72. The trail crosses at a good spot for seeing traffic. Once on the other side, it is back to single track again. Just a little ways and there is another forest clearing project. Thanks to Sally Wilhelm, there is a row of trees left beside the trail to keep the sun off on a hot day. I remember when she went clear to Lansing to fight the battle to leave the trees beside the trail standing. Taking away the trees really makes this area look different.

Not too far and I get to the popple trees that are a produce of a past cutting. They are really thick and the trail is almost hidden. Valley Road (paved) appears and

and out onto a gravel road.

Another good cantering spot. A pretty creek crosses under the road and another screeching halt. The size of this creek always amazes me because it comes from the big spring you see to your right. It reminds me of Big Springs in the U.P. near Manistique. It is so close to M-72, I can't help wonder why someone hasn't capitalized on it. I could have watered my horse on either side, but he is young and water is not his thing. I would have to pick a fight and I don't like to pick fights when I ride alone.

Right after this creek, the trail turns left and in just a short while it brings you into Kalkaska Camp. A dry came (no river, but a hand pump), but a pretty peaceful camp. There is also a well there for generators.

KALKASKA
TO
GOOSE CREEK

U.S. 131

CO 671

Maniste
Lake

SEELEY RD   State Rd

SKY VAL
RAM

M72   (NEW)

KALKASKA CAMP
(old)
KALKASKA

US 131

Wagonschutz
Rd

M72

M66

Key to trail markers
1965 - - - - - - - - -
1969 0 0 0 0 0 0 0
1977 > > > > > > >
1985 X X X X X X
1994 H H H H H H

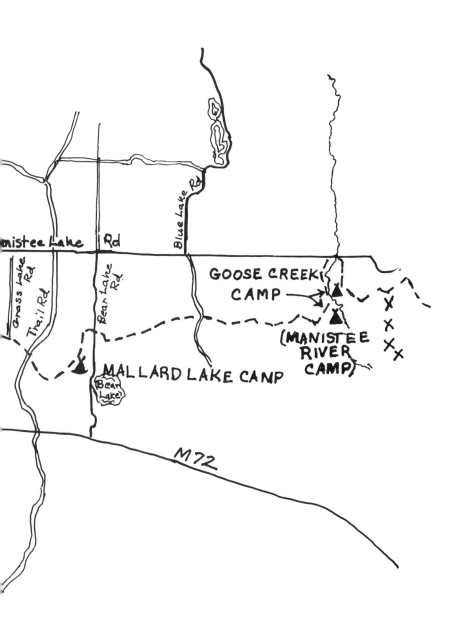

KALKASKA TO GOOSE CREEK

I doubt if this stretch is anybody's favorite. It starts out all right - a single path through some pines that have grown too big, then just a nice pathway through the woods. In about 2 miles you get to U.S. 131, north of Kalkaska. The trail goes straight across and on through the woods for another 3 miles. When you emerge onto a two track a post tells you to turn left. This is hard to follow because the trees are so far back from the two-track where the signs have been stapled. As you cross a gravel road you will see some blue paint on a cyclone fence that goes around a gas well. At the end of that two-track you will turn right and head east toward the swamp.

Up the road a little ways is a steel gate chained shut. Right beside it is a place for a horse to walk through, if you have a dependable horse. He really can't get hurt on it, but he might think it is too narrow. The road continues on, graveled and wide enough for a big pickup. A nice bridge big enough for the pickup to go over covers a nice creek. There is some gravel on the right side of the bridge on both sides of the creek, making it a nice place to water a horse and then cross the creek.

Further on there have been some big 8 x 8 planks lined up so a truck could drive over them. I couldn't believe this trail. The last time I crossed it, about 5 years ago, there were six or seven bridges with steps up and down. Just around the corner I saw why the road was so nice; someone has taken up residence of that old cabin. He has even built the cutest outhouse out of logs. It looks like a mini-log cabin out back with a board walk leading to it. Seems like a weird place to live if you ask me. No creek by the house, just swamp and bugs.

From then on, the trail was the old single path down the gasline, until you turn right and get over next to the swamp. This part has some kind of black fiberglass laid on the bottom with loads of gravel dumped on by a dump truck. Another nice bridge over a creek that a truck can drive over and then another steel gate with a walkway for a horse beside it. Was I surprised! What had happened to all those bridges. This is by far safer and should hold up for a long time.

Once out of the swamp we are on a regular gravel road. At the corner the trail turns right and goes through some beautiful hardwoods. At the corner the trail turns left onto Meyers Rd. This is the home of the Lost Creek Sky Ranch that used to be a dude ranch when the trail riders first started to ride here. This is the ranch that Sally rode to with her sore mouth and sore arm. That swamp is the one Jane

Guinn thought she fell into when she, Sally and Tony rode through it in the dark. I was scared there by myself in the daylight, I can't imagine riding through it in the dark what with all the murky, slimy things that must live in there.

Meyers Road is the beginning of a long stretch of road riding. I would say at least 8 to 10 miles of it before you enter the woods again. You will pass two creeks that are possible to water a horse at. The first one has almost dried up on dry years, but the second one is good and easy to get into. I remember standing in this creek with Sue Hoogesteger, now Kesslar. She was sitting on her three year old mare, relaxing while her mare drank, and I saw the legs start to buckle. I did not have time to say, "Sue, I think your horse is going to lay down." She just crumbled right down into that water and Sue had to step off into cold, crotch deep water and make her horse get up. That mare developed the habit of trying to lay down in every creek she drank at.

The trail leaves the road and goes straight east into the woods. This is the best 10 miles of this whole stretch. Nice open hardwoods with some hills to wind around. About 3 miles of this and you come to a paved road. The trail follows it just a little ways and then crosses. Not long into this section and you come to railroad history. Old stumps rotting everywhere tell us there used to be a beautiful pine forest here. Long level mounds that wind around the woods tell us those are man made and probably involved some horse labor also. Logs were hauled along these old railroad beds. Some of the houses on Sixth Street were made from the lumber from this area. The one funeral home that has each room made with a different kind of wood can tell you where the lumber came from in this area. If you look carefully, you can find holes where lumber cabins used to sit. There are big ones for the bunk houses, and smaller ones for the cook shack and storage houses. A lot of people eat their lunches right here —with the ghosts of the past.

A ghost got my horse right here once and he ran six miles back to Meyers Rd., but that is another story.

A bit further and you come to the used to be birches. There used to be solid birch trees through here and they were so close there wasn't any underbrush. This was the favorite lunch spot. But they started to decay because of old age, so they were harvested. Now the area is a blackberry heaven.

More beautiful woods with an open spot here and there. My daughter and I saw a bear itching his back on a wild cherry tree in one of these open areas one fine day. We watched him itch, then he stopped to look at us. He went back to itching and then decided to run in the other direction. We stood perfectly still until he was out of sight, not quite believing our eyes, but in the back of our minds we were ready to run our horses in his opposite direction. There are so many black berries through there, it makes a good place for a bear to fill his tummy.

On down the trail a little further is where I passed three motorcyclists pushing their bikes up the dirt hill. My horse galloped past them, scaring them out of their wits. They yelled at me some obscenities and reved up their motors to try to catch me. I had not had any sleep the night before because of a dying foal, and I had ridden from Shecks all the way to Goose Creek in a 50 mile competitive ride. I thought I was so tired I couldn't ride another mile, but when those guys started chasing me, my horse's adrenalin shot up and so did mine and we had power to spare. We galloped the rest of the way to the gravel road. They stopped a friend of mine who came along later and told her if they ever caught up with me, they were going to shoot that *&^%$ horse right out from underneath me. I have had so many motorcycles scare my horses, that for once I thought I was really smart to finally scare one of them.

Once at the gravel road, you are almost at camp. A path takes you across a field and through some pines and there you are at the edge of the great Manistee River. There is a special place made for horses to enter and cross, and climb out of the river on the other side. You are now in one of the favorite camps on the Shore to Shore Riding and Hiking Trail —Goose Creek. You can park your rig along the river or out in the open field. The pump is out in the field.

163

Cory McCallister leaving Goose Creek

Megan Gee & Rhoda Ritter arriving at Goose Creek

GOOSE CREEK
TO
FOUR MILE

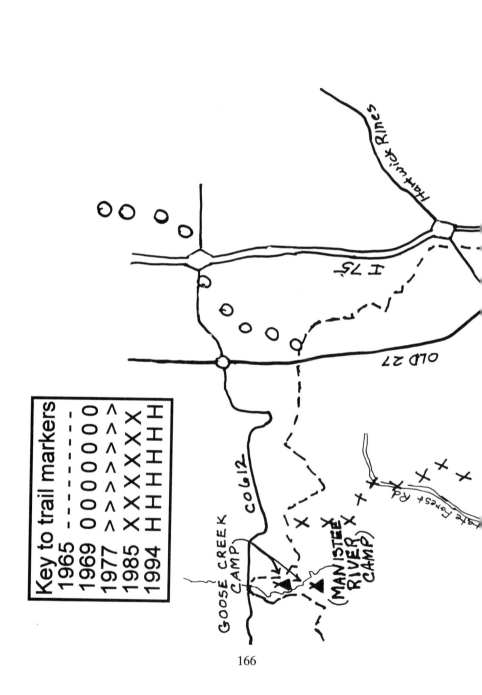

Key to trail markers
1965 - - - - - - -
1969 O O O O O O O
1977 > > > > > > >
1985 X X X X X X X
1994 H H H H H H H

Hartwick Pines

I 75

OLD 27

CO 612

GOOSE CREEK CAMP

MANISTEE RIVER (CAMP)

State Forest Rd.

166

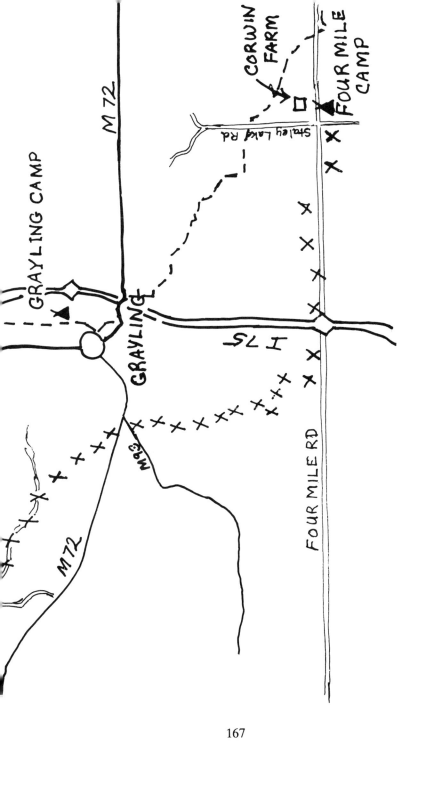

GOOSE CREEK TO FOUR MILE

We parked the rig in the big open field at the Goose Creek Trail Camp on the east side of the Manistee River. Our intention, on this beautiful summer day, was to ride the trail east to Four Mile Camp. The trail had been changed to the west of Grayling and would be new to us. Saddles tightened on and lunches packed on the saddle bags, we start out toward the Manistee River Road.

It is quite obvious where the trail crosses the pavement and dips down into the ditch because of the erosion. The well defined path weaves through jack pine and open areas of grass to the bottom of a big hill where there are quite a few choices to make our way to the top. At the top is the old foundation of the fire tower that was there when the trail was first started. A little ride along the ridge and the path takes us down. A few roots have survived the horses hooves and try to trip our horses. At the bottom the path is very sandy and dusty for the third and fourth horse. We trot along studying the growth of the white pine that were planted in rows some years back. They sure grow fast, I remember when there was nothing here. (Wasn't that just yesterday?) We cross a two track in a hurry because we hear something loudly motorized approaching. Two hooded drivers come at us racing side by side on those little four wheeled toys. They buzz right past us on down the road, never even knowing they were being watched. (Oh well, everyone should have some kind of hobby).

The trail takes a two track for a ways then comes into an open area where there is a split. We decide (unlike Robert Frost) to take the trail more trodden with no leaves of black. There are a few wild cherry and scrub oak leaves in the other trail because it is the old trail that only gets used by people who camp in Goose Creek and ride into the town of Frederick for a very delicious meal and drinks. It used to take people to Elk Hill, but a new route was developed in 1995 from Luzerne. There is a sign there telling us Four Mile Camp is to the right. It is a fun single path to trot on, twisty and turny, but enough open areas to be able to see what was up ahead. It climbs upwards some and we see more hardwoods. A few miles of this and we come to a regular back country road of graded sand. A good cantering place and we canter for miles. The trail turns into the woods again and is a nice single track through the normal scrub oak, popple, and pine for Michigan.

We spy something ahead that looks like a baricade. As we approach we realize we have entered a army bivwak area. Contidina fence is right across the trail and there are men milling about, wearing army fatigues, carrying guns, waiting for something to happen. We are told that we can't pass through the area because they are on manuvers and they expect to be attached any minute.

There can be no turning back for us because our trailer has been moved to Four Mile Camp. We pretend we are going back until we are out of their sight, then we take out our campass and head west. After a few minutes we head south, and after quite a few minutes and a lot of brush, we head back east to pick up the trail. For the next few miles we encounter jeeps, six tracks, telephone wire across our path, weird yellow pieces of plastic hanging from bushes (we learn later that these are chemical testers) and a very torn up woods. We are very relieved to hear the traffic from M-72 in the distance.

When we arrive at M-72, the half-way point, we recognize the stop light and party store about one mile west of Grayling where Military Road branches off from M-72. We cross rapidly, because it is summer and the traffic is heavy. Yipes, what is this bog doing next to the highway and why does the trail go through the middle of it. We test the water puddles and they seem to have a firm bottom. Carefully we wade, horse knee deep, to Military Road, maybe a half a mile. The trail follows the road toward the army camp (west) about a mile before turning left toward a recreational area. I look for the trail markers that take us across the field, but they lead us right into the parking lot of the lodge. A little path leads down to the pond on the left, across from the baseball diamond, and I can't find a sign saying not to water your horses in the pond. The approach looks like horses have drank here before us, so we each take our turn letting our horses drink their fill. (You can do this if you keep on riding your horse.) To get out of the parking area, we are shown the way by our friendly sign of the horse shoe/human foot print tacked to the light pole along side the lodge.

We are led around a gate and into a sparsely wooded area with a maze of trails going every which way. I look around trying to find the trailer park that used to be full to bursting at this time every other summer. I see a sign that says: Camp Closed.

We trot on south, slowing to a walk every little ways because of the deep sand. This used to be quite a busy place for O.R.V.'s. The land is pretty well dug up with only grass able to grow close to the trees. The trail is tough for a horse because of the deep sand. Tendons can be pulled easily on a tired horse, so we take our time. It is a pretty woods to ride through; huge oaks with so much shade that only quack grass can grow amongst the years and years of acorn fertilized ground. Finally we start seeing wild cherry in the distance and we know we're getting close to Four Mile Road.

At Four Mile Road (four miles south of Grayling) we turn east and ride along the pavement, studying the viaduct over I-75 in the not far enough distance. In the past a log truck always chose to cross about the time I was right in the middle of that viaduct. We canter and get their too quickly. No log truck has crossed. That means one is due. There is some kind of a business that uses a lot of logs about a mile east on Four Mile. I dismount. I feel better leading my 900 pound animal, with the brain of a three year old human, who's first instinct is to self destruct. Oh my God. Here comes one. Maybe if I throw my body down on the pavement in front of him, he will slow down. Never mind, I'll just start running and see if I can outrun the bugger. Panting heavily, I run down the viaduct and onto the grass of the shoulder. I am safe again. The rest of my crew have more stable mounts. (I seem to always get the weird ones.)

"Only Four More Miles", becomes a true statement. The trail leads us parrell to the pavement, but back in the woods amongst scrub oaks, and some hard woods. We come out to the pavement at the railroad tracks but get to re-enter the woods right after. About two miles on the left side of the road and the trail takes us across to the right side. There are a row of houses here so we have to ride the shoulder. The last little way before camp we get to ride in the woods again, along the road. We cross and paved road and a sign says "Four Mile Trail Camp". We made it. Now to find the rig.

Four Mile Camp is quite spacious with two tracks taking rigs to the rear of the woods: jackpines and blueberry bushes. The pump at this camp is very good and the water is delicious. The driver of our rig says he has had a very peaceful day. We begin to tell him about the army bivwak and the log truck while the horses wait anxiously to be unsaddled and allowed to eat grass.

Norm Draper

Don Edwards

FOUR MILE
TO
LUZERNE

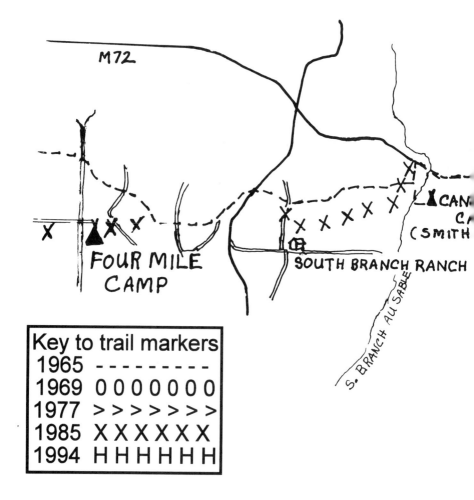

M72

CAN
C
(SMITH

FOUR MILE
CAMP

SOUTH BRANCH RANCH

S. BRANCH AU SABLE

Key to trail markers
1965 - - - - - - - - -
1969 O O O O O O O
1977 > > > > > > >
1985 X X X X X X
1994 H H H H H H

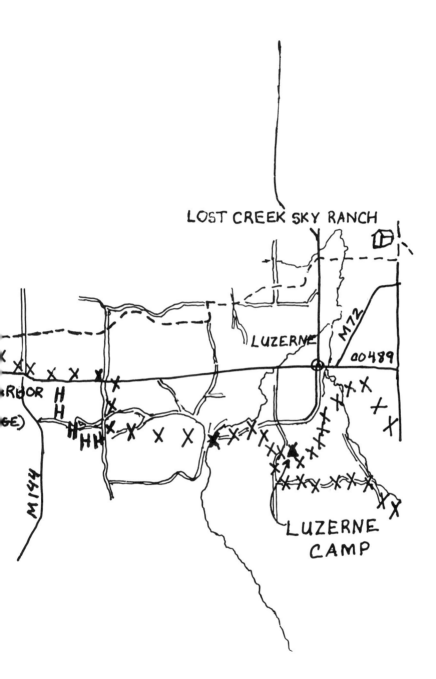

LOST CREEK SKY RANCH

LUZERNE

M72

00489

RBOR

(GE)

M144

LUZERNE
CAMP

FOUR MILE TO LUZERNE

I wake up to rain drops on the camper roof. Not loud rain drops, just small quiet ones. That's not ideal, but it's O.K. The trail I have to ride today can be nasty on a hot day, so a warm mist will be fine. I pull my big long tailed, yellow, plastic coated rain coat from the closet and stuff the pockets with M&M's, roasted almonds, an extra bottle of Coke, a necessary sandwich, and paper towel to wipe the rain off my glasses periodicly. My rain hat keeps the rain off the glasses while walking, but every once in a while a leafy branch seems to surprise me and I hate not being able to see. Next, from the closet, comes the vinyl saddle cover I made especially for my english/endurance saddle. Finally, I'm all set for a leisure day of feasting in the forest!

To ride east out Four Mile I must go right as I ride out of camp. It is a wide, back country road with little traffic once you pass the Jellystone Park a little way from camp. I'm not sure how the mood is in today's time, but in the past Jellystone would let trail riders pay for hot showers and let us dump holding tanks at their park.

Now that I am past the park driveway, I think I'll try a little trot to see if all my goodies stay in my pockets or bounce out. Wow! I am surprised to see that a fire has burned the jack pines on both sides of the road. Must have been fairly recent because their is very little under growth coming back. I trot to the end of the wide road (about a mile) and check my pockets. Didn't lose a thing.

A two track now takes me into the jack pine forest with blueberry bushes amongst the blue scrub ground cover. Never did learn if that stuff was a plant or a spiny moss. I know it gets mighty brittle when it is dry. The sand is a little deep here, making my horse work a little harder. I'll let him walk. I study the jack pine and try to figure why it was ever planted. Someone told me that G. Mennen Williams had the CCC boys plant jack pine all over Michigan to reforest what was cut down by the lumber companies. He must not have realized that they are a very crooked, scraggly, short lived, ugly tree. Every once in a while I can find a good, straight, young, jack pine. Makes me wonder if they weren't so crowded, would they make a better tree. I also see a scrub oak scattered amongst the pines. Ground becomes a little firmer, time to trot again; only a couple of miles to the first paved road.

In crossing the paved road, I have now entered Death Valley. This stretch was named by the group that created the trail. On a hot day with the temperatures in the high 80's or low 90's, this 5 or 6 mile stretch can seem unbearable. The pines hold back the breezes and the gnats horde over you like a cloud of vultures, each diving in for his share of your blood. I can remember riding through here when they were so bad I would spray bug repellant on my face until it ran off and they would still dive into it and get caught so I would have to flick them off with my finger. The best way to survive was a branch of leaves, if you could get a scrub oak to break, and swish it back and forth in front of your face like a fan. People started creating all kinds of ear covers for their horses that seemed to help the poor beast so he could continue on his way without shaking his ears off. Today, I do not have a problem; the rain keeps the bugs away and also firms up the sand.

About a mile from the paved road the new trail turns me to the right. Not too far and a single path turns me back east. I like this stretch. There are some hills, and hardwoods, and wild life. A good time to get out some M&M's and relax. I see a doe and her fawn off to the right on a hill side. They are far enough away to not be frightened, just curious. I stop crunching the peanuts, not wanting to break the silence. This is the nice part about riding alone on a rainy day. I ride along, munching, wondering what it would be like if I were a deer. Summers would be great, but I don't think I would like to be a deer in hunting season or winter. My horse hears something and tries to find it, pointing his ears where his eyes are looking. I find it. A porcupine climbing slowly up a tree. We continue. I finish the M&M's and take a few sips of pop. These screw on tops on the plastic bottles come in real handy when a person only wants a few sips!

The trail starts decending and I recognize the rows of white pines I have to ride through to get to M-72. Not very far, just across a corner, but they sure have grown big and they slap on my rain coat and soak my feet. The trail crosses M-72 here and takes a little dirt road that takes us to Smith Bridge. It is quite necessary to take this route, because we have to cross the south branch of the AuSable River. It is very nice to have this little bridge down by the river with a parking lot and outhouse. If it weren't here, we'd have to cross the river via the highway and being at the bottom of a long hill from the east, traffic gets to going pretty fast across the river. I think the only people who might use this parking lot would be canoeist and fishermen. I hope they can keep it open for us. It is a wonderful place to water a horse and cool him down (on a hot day). Today, my horse gets to drink about five swallows and then rest tied to a tree by the outhouse. I get to eat my sandwich; funny how I got hungry all of a sudden and the sandwich looks pretty tasty. The pop is still cold in my insulated pocket pad with a now unfrozen ice pack. As I eat my lunch I think back (I always think best eating) to the many times I have ridden to this spot so hot I thought I couldn't go any further, but after cooling myself and my horse in that beautiful river, I would feel like a new person. I wonder how many hundreds of people, this particular place on the river has revived. This I believe is where Doc Lannen was pushed in by Rex and taught the trail riders way to cool off in a river.

Today, I do not have to cool off, I am just right. I water my horse again and look around for a post. My horse is not only weird, he is tall, but he is stump trained. I mount. Ahh! That wet saddle cover is refreshing. Better the cover than my saddle. I take the trail up out of the parking lot east past the outhouse. Ride along the road a bit and they climb up a hill into the woods. The trail will go parrell to M-72 but it is back far enough in the woods so very little traffic sounds reach me. Right along in here is where Tony had his race with Les. I can see why it was hairy. I approach a cutting where the under brush is half grown trees. The trail is single and winding. It is also blinding because I can't see around the corners, and the wet leaves keep slapping my glasses. I finally put the glasses in my shirt pocket. Now I can trot through here. Soon the trail enters some more jack pines planted in rows. I remember right through here, a few years back, with a girl friend of mine who was having trouble with her under wear. (I'm sure we can all relate.) I finally told her to get rid of them. She took out her swiss army knife and slit the sides and pulled them off like a pamper, never even stopping her horse. " What do I do with them now?" she asked. "Hang them on a branch of a jack pine, so other people will know what to do with bad underwear," I told her. So she did. I remember riding through there about 2 years after that and they were still hanging there. I, then, picked them off and what I did with them is another story.

I pick up the pace to a trot and reach the paved road. Cross it and continue trotting. Just a little ways and I reach M-72. Cross it and go down a single path through some planted white pine. These are still small and I can see quite a way so I put on my glasses again. (Good thing I brought that paper towel). This area leads through some open, grassy, areas amongst taller jack pines and then the woods turns into hardwoods for about 4 or 5 miles. I trot the trail to the hardwoods, then I settle down for some more animal watching and munching. This time the roasted almonds. My pace is rewarded with the sighting of a couple of deer. These two do not stick around. I come across a tree struck by lightening, split right to the ground, and then about a 8 inch groove dug in the ground extend about 15 feet from the base of the tree. That must have been one mean bolt of power.

The single trail connects with a two-track and turns left. This tells me that I am not too far from old M-144. We decend a long hill and come out onto a gravel road, turn left, and find a river. This is old M-144 and the river is called Big Creek. There is evidence of a man made pathway to allow horses to enter the river on one side and walk out the other. It is only about 30 inches max in the middle, and about two horse lengths across, but it is the last good water. Luzerne is four miles from here and the pump is very hard to get any water out of, being so deep.

My horse drinks his fill and decides he wants to get out, so we head on east up the road. About a 1/4 of a mile the blue trail takes me into the woods on the right. The part of the trail always seems so long because they tried to put it on the ridges to avoid erosion. Seems like it goes in circles. It is pretty, with hardwoods and some smaller bushes. Witch Hazel bushes I believe. These are an interesting bush, really, because they flower in the fall and drop their seeds in the spring. The skin refresher witch hazel is made from this bush.

The trail comes out onto a dirt road right across from the entrance to Luzerne Camp. This is a beautiful camp. Big shady hardwoods, lets it seem spacious. It is on a high hill just a couple miles south of the town of Luzerne. There is a small camping area with a gate for the use of larger groups. The campsites in the overflow area are pull through so it takes a bit of co-operation to get very many rigs in there. In the overflow area there is also a deep well for generators. There are always a lot of cicada's in this camp. Their empty body shells can be found at the bottom of most of the trees. For those of you who have never heard of the cicada before, I'm sure you have heard it. On hot dry days in the summer you hear it making it's mating call which is a high pitched whine that gets real loud then drops off to nothing. To anyone with Tininitus (ringing in the ears) it really bothers the ears. The cicada lives in the roots of trees and when it is time to metamorphose, it climbs up the trunk of the tree, fastens it feet securely to the bark, and proceeds to split it's skin down the back, allowing the adult cicada to climb out. After the adult dries it's wings for a few hours, it starts it's mating call. I love to hunt for the shells of the cicada nymph in this camp and have found many handfuls of them. They are a light brown sorta transparent looking bug about the size of a bumble bee. They are totally hollow inside with their eyes still open on their faces. Really interesting to a nature nut!

LUZERNE
TO
MCKINLEY

MCKINLEY
TO
SOUTH BRANCH

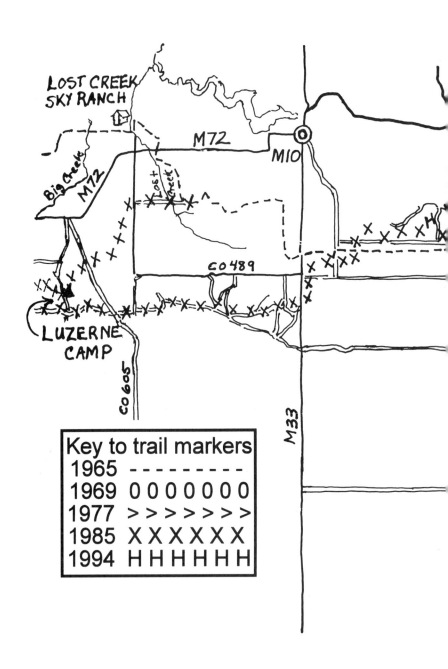

LOST CREEK
SKY RANCH

M72

M10

Big Creek

M72

Lost Creek

CO 489

LUZERNE
CAMP

CO 605

M33

Key to trail markers
1965 - - - - - - - -
1969 0 0 0 0 0 0 0
1977 > > > > > > >
1985 X X X X X X
1994 H H H H H H

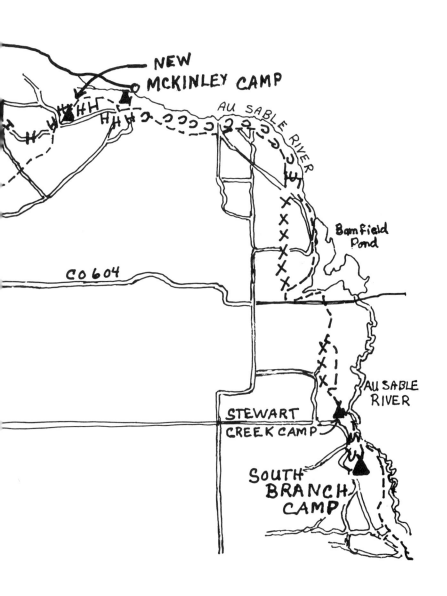

LUZERNE TO MCKINLEY

Today's trail is one of my favorite, favorite; the trees are leafy and the territory wild and free. The trail from Four Mile to Luzerne is woodsy and pleasant, but I know I am never very far from M-72. Today's trail will parrellel a secondary paved road that turns into gravel - 489. I take one long look at Luzerne Camp as I ride out. The huge beech and maple are so thick they cover the forest floor with so much shade nothing else can grow there. The early morning's sun manages to shoot a few beams through, that go all the way to the ground uninterrupted. There they find a thick layer of leaves and a few ferns. This picture would make a beautiful mural for a wall. There used to be two wigwam shaped outhouses with cedar shingles all the way to the ground that I always thought were very unique. They have been replaced with the same shaped ones found in all the camps today.

I bid the pump goodbye as I pass, envying it because it gets to spend all its time in such a beautiful, most of the time, peaceful place. The trail is a single path to the east just past the pump. As we decend the hill, the forest becomes the usual mixed Michigan forest. Every once in a while I catch the glimpse of a deer. Bluejays are squaking and telling them I am coming. It is just a few miles to the Luzerne Bridge. The open areas just before it show signs of people camping there. The fire pits are full of charred wood and left over, half burned human refuse. Sure don't have to wonder what species used this part of the forest last.

The bridge looks a little slippery and my weird horse is apprehensive so I will get off and lead him. I want to be able to look around at the beauty of things, without having to guide a horse who doesn't want to be guided. He is much more relaxed as we clip-clop across the wooden walkway through this magic swamp with me going first. Magic, because there are not any visual signs how this bridge came to be here. Not a tree or bush was visably moved to make way for this quarter mile long boardwalk for horses and man. This is a two part bridge with solid ground in the middle that allows the horse to get a firm foot hold, and a place to enter the stream (east branch of the AuSable) for a drink. I feel the water and it is really cold. I notice a big red pine has been hit by lightening and split from top to bottom. I wonder why this particular was hit and not the ones right beside it. I lead my horse onto the second section of the bridge. We cross over a little bridge and there is a little incline. The sun manages to filter down some sunbeams that make the water sparkle as it ripples along. There are some huge cedar trees in this swamp. Looks like something out of Cinderella. Definetly another world. At the end of the boardwalk is a water trough with water running out of a pvc pipe that has been driven back into the hillside. My understanding is this water has never been tested for human consumtion, but I have been known to drink it on a hot day.

I find a place on the bank to mount my horse and we head on up the pathway that leads us back up to the normal type of woods. There is a sign that points to a scenic overlook. It is a serene view of treetops in a small valley. A birdseye view,

185

you might say.

Back on the trail, the hardwoods disappear and we trot through open areas with jackpines, scrub oak and grassy areas. Now we come to the hard part; small hills with round rocks on the sand that makes hill climbing hard for a horse. There is a nice, level two track going in the same direction I am and I have never understood why they made this trail climb these hills unless for one reason: the motorcycle deterant and if so, they were right. Too many miles of this stuff before we finally come to a paved road. It is called Mapes Road by name, and 489 by number. We (my horse and I) cross it and trot a little ways and another paved road. It is still 489 but now it is called Zimowski Road. Some more hills and with rocks and sand to contend with. Three or four miles of this and we pop up out of a valley onto a busy paved road. This is M-33, just south of Mio. We cross, and pick up the single path in some woods with more hardwoods than pines. Not even a mile and we again climb up out of a low, piney area onto a gravel road. This is again M-489 heading east. I just remembered that this was the area that burned about 10 or 15 years ago. The DNR planned a burn to make the jack pine cones open and reforest the area for the Kirkland Warbler, a song bird near extinction. The wind got ahold of the fire and burned a lot more than the projected plan. It sure looks nice now. (If you want to watch the jack pine cones open, lay them up close to a campfire and as the wax coating melts, they open and this allows the seeds to fall out.)

We cross the dirt road and trot on down a two track through my favorite kind of trees; hardwoods! About a mile in from the road is the water hole - - a shallow place in the woods that always has water in it. Also frogs! It is about halfway between the two camps and at one time the only place to water. There used to be a "john" just around the bend of the path.

The rest of the way into McKinley is mostly hardwoods and good solid pathway. This was where there were too many logs left and the first trip through caused many shin bumps. There was a work bee formed to remove most of them. Everything is so clean. Not a sign of the human except the pathway and blue dots. On a cool day, the trail is perfect for trotting, but on a hot humid day, it can get pretty close down under the trees. You can look up and see the trees moving on the tops and know there must be a breeze up there, but it cannot get down to the forest floor. When this occurs, it can be a very long trail.

This day is perfect and I can trot our little eight mile an hour trot. Whoa! Thank God for manes! A startled deer lets out a snort just before it jumps out of a clump of young maples and runs off in the opposite direction. Did you ever wonder how much power it takes a horse to jump so fast in such a flash of time. It's got to be measured in more than horse-power. Maybe we could call it "jet" horse power. I recover my seat and gather up the reins and start trotting again.

This trail gets kinda mind boggling through here. It has changed quite a few times to protect the environment. It used to go right beside a tree with a little cross under it. A man who had lived and hunted this area all his life was creamated and his ashes were buried under a huge tree. The whole area around that grave was cut down, but they left the tree with the cross under it.

The forest opens up the closer we get to McKinley camp with more pines and less hard woods. Somewhere along here is a water trough with a big long pvc pipe coming out of a hill. A small trickle of water keeps the water fresh. The biggest problem is keeping the water trough from leaking. It is wooden.

I decide to take the old road down a long, slopeing grade to camp. I soon learn this is not a good idea. There are mogels (ups and downs made by snow machines and ORV's.) I notice the hillsides are nothing but sand. There are signs that humans have camped here and tested their equipment by trying to climb the hills. There is erosion everywhere I look. No wonder the DNR just cringes when we ask for more public land to play on.

The blue trail crosses my road and I decide to take the single pathway into McKinley. More jack pine are showing up so I know I am getting close. I dip down onto a dirt road, jump back up the bank on the other side and this tells me I am almost there.

When I arrive at the two-track that goes straight between rows and rows of red pines, I know I am in camp. In this camp people would drive their rigs in and back up to the pines. Everybody parked side by side. They have since enlarged the camp and made a circle drive. There is also a deep well pump in the new part up on the hill. The old pump is straight past the baricade to the left on the hill, a little ways beyond the toilets. The pump is kinda unique because a pipe takes the pumped water underground to the bottom of the hill where it used to fill a water tank. Water tanks have been discouraged on trail rides because of the spread of disease. It is much safer to water out of your own pail. I sure hope no one has dismantled the pump, I am dying of thirst, and this water is so-o-o good.

187

The AuSable River

MCKINLEY TO SOUTH BRANCH

If you only have one day to ride the Michigan Riding and Hiking Trail, ride this segment between McKinley and South Branch.

McKinley Camp is really way out in the wild country. It is easiest to get to from Mio. County road 602 heads east from the main street of Mio, directly across the stop light from the intersection where M-72 stops and then turns left (north). 602 follows the power line that follows the AuSable River. About 9 miles from Mio there is a sign reading McKinley Trail Camp, and an arrow that points left. A two-track leads you into camp, about a mile. Back in the early 70's we rode across Michigan on the blue trail with 6 early teenagers. It was the second week of August and we were riding east to west. We had to jump our own rig, leave it, take the car back to ride for the day, then at night, take the rig back and get the car. The roads in this area are very poorly marked and the camp was not marked at all.. It took us until 11:00 AM to find a place to park the rig and get back to the horses. The trail is especially long and especially beautiful, so we did not get into camp until after supper time. By the time we went back for the car and both were in camp, it was nearly 11:00 PM. This experience taught us to read maps, keep close tabs on the odometer, and keep the compass out the window. We did make it all the way and we rode every day. It was probably one of the most memorable trips across, mainly because we had to find the way without the help of hoof prints in the sand, and people leading caravans of rigs with us just following. The kids were great, the weather was great, and the trip was great.

The trail out of McKinley goes east from the electric well at the top of the hill. It winds down and up small hills, and through a slightly mucky area. The forest is piney and oaky, with grass amongst the trees. There are 19 bridges, of some sort or fashion, on this section you will ride today and before you get two miles, you will have to cross two of them. Some of them are layers of plywood, some are logs nailed crossways on logs, and some are wooden planks with side rails. Usually they are safe unless some beaver family has decided to build a dam down stream and the back flood waters cover the bridge, which has been the case a number of times. The trail stays on the river side of 602 for a couple of miles, although you won't see the river. When you come to a dirt road, it is 602 and you will cross straight across it. The trail is single path and not too winding through beautiful mixed woods. In about 1/2 a mile the trail crosses another dirt road. The same distance and you cross another dirt road and head for the river. For the next six miles you will ride along the river. You will not see any sign of human residency along here, just wild country. There are eagles and osprey that fish the river to watch for, plus wild turkey, deer and the usual woodsy inhabitants. The trail has big, round rocks imbedded in it and needs some attention from the driver of the horse to get through here without a stone bruise. I'm not sure if you will find any place to water along the AuSable. Most of the places that were used in the olden days have been barricaded to prevent further damage to the banks. There will be creek crossing that you can use to water your horse. The way I ride this trail is to trot wherever I don't see river and walk whenever I do.

About five miles of river riding brings you to the 4001 Bridge. This used to be a beautiful place to water your horse, but it is now closed. Right across the road is a parking area and a canoe landing. It is possible to walk down a cement pathway to the water's edge and give your horse a chance to drink. I would not suggest doing this if people are hauling canoes up and out of there because it is real close to their roller. There is also a outhouse in the parking area.

It isn't very far after this, the trail pulls you off the river to ride in an area that is a little more open. In the beginning, the trail rode the steep hills along this part, but the erosion really damaged the forest. It is much better for the woods where it is now. It is still very pretty, and wild, and a good place to trot.

In about three miles the trail comes to a big cliff overlooking Alcona reservoir. This is a result of a dam about a mile down river. This is a good place to tie up your horse, eat lunch, and absorb the view. I'd say the cliff is about 300 feet high. There used to be an eagles nest on the right way off on the horizon about three miles away. There is a campground straight across the pond on a little point of land that fingers out into the river and another one to the left on our side of the river.

From here you leave the river again and follow a well worn pathway for about a mile, over a little creek and on up the ravine to the Curtisville Road. The trail goes to the left at this point, but there is a really well worn path to the right about half a mile to the Curtisville Store. Curtisville is one party store and about a dozen houses. You can find drinks, snacks, and goodies at this store. Just tie your horse at the chewed up trees across the road; there isn't anyplace to tie them at the store.

Once back on the right trail again, it will be about 4 miles of woods riding before you will come to another high bank on the AuSable River. This is a nice to camp so you will probably run into people taking advantage of the beautiful scene and the peace and quiet. About a half mile from here is Stewarts Creek. When you come to this clear spot on the banks of the AuSable River with a creek running into the river down the bank from you, and a wooden stairway down to the river for canoeist to climb up for a rest, please realize this is one of the first camps used by .the Michigan Trail Riders on their first crossings. The trail used to go down to the creek and cross at the mouth of the river, climbing the bank on the other side. If you care to walk down there, you will see the terrible erosion that it caused. The present trail takes you across the creek on a nice bridge with a water tank along side for your horse to drink out of, and then up the hill at an angle which is not as destructive as going straight up and down.

The old trail used to take us along side the river all the way into South Branch Camp. The river started to undercut the trail and parts of it would cave into the river, making it a very treacherous trail indeed. So now the way to camp is through the woods, along the road a little way, and then into camp.

South Branch is a beautiful campground nestled amongst white pines and big oaks. The open areas are grassy. There are designated campsites with pits for cooking, a good pump with delicious water, and outhouses. There is also a large overflow area for large groups for which a permit is required. Just a little hike around the hill and you can cool off in the South Branch of the AuSable River. If you want to follow that river just a little ways, you will come to the fork where it enters into the main AuSable.

Smith Bridge

The 4001 Bridge

SOUTH BRANCH
TO
OSCODA

SOUTH BRANCH
TO
TAWAS CITY

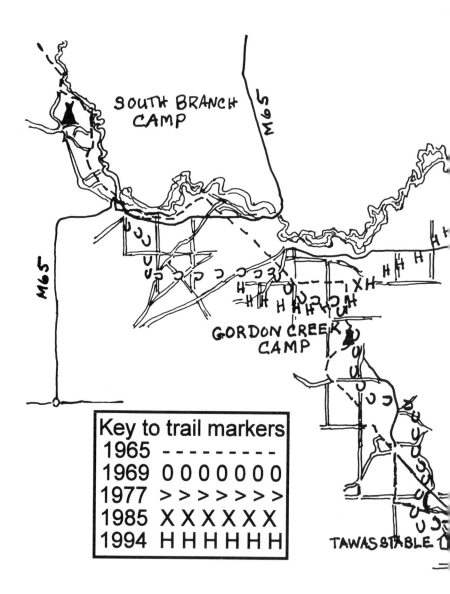

SOUTH BRANCH CAMP

M65

M65

GORDON CREEK CAMP

Key to trail markers
1965 - - - - - - - - - -
1969 O O O O O O O
1977 > > > > > > >
1985 X X X X X X
1994 H H H H H H

TAWAS STABLE

OLD ORCHARD
PARK

OSCODA

TAWAS
LAKE

LAKE
HURON

TAWAS
CITY

SOUTH BRANCH TO OSCODA

South Branch Camp is right at the top of the list of my favorite campsites. The camp itself (described in the McKinley to South Branch segment) seems so clean because the ground is either covered by grass or leaves and there isn't any underbrush. The trees are all tall so you feel like you are camped underneath a big canopy. I have never found it to be buggy except for one weird time when four of us women were camping there. We had ridden out all day along the river and had just gotten back and had our horses unsaddled and picketed. We sat down to have a cold pop when a swarm of big, black, flies started to land on the horses and bite them so badly they were lunging and pulling on the lines. One horse was laying down and rolling, then getting up and kicking out his hind heels, then rolling again. They looked like the kind of fly we find in our houses and I could not understand why they were attaching our horses and us. We soaked the horses with horse-fly spray and put blankets on them. We finally put them in the horse trailers. The people were not being so tortured, but we did have to spray ourselves to be left alone. By the time we had accomplished all this, which probably took up almost an hour, the flies disappeared as suddenly as they had come.

When you are camping in the camp itself, you do not see any signs of a river. But, about a quarter of a mile around and down the back of camp is the South Branch of the AuSable. It is clear and clean and has quiet a current, but it is only about 2 feet deep. If you follow the trail along it you will find a place where the trail crosses to an open field. Keep following the trail and you will come to the banks of the big AuSable. Here the river is deep and swift and beautiful if you know how to swim. If you are on horseback, just keep following the trail and it will take you along the river on a two-track back to the where the blue trail takes you to South Branch. This might be a mile depending on if you are starting your ride on a sunny morning, or if you have ridden all day and you decide to take a short ride bareback on a sweaty horse - then it seems like 10 miles.

There are many trails to ride out of camp in any direction, plus the soft dirt roads that are square miles and all marked with forest posts and numbers. There is a party store about 2 1/2 miles from camp on the corner of Rollaway Road and M-65 that supplies everything a camper might need.

The trail to Oscoda is just about all single path. It leaves climbing the hill at the end of the overflow camping area and follows the ridge. There has been a lot of erosion and deep furrowing along here due to four, three, and two wheeled motor vehicles. That only lasts about two miles before the horse trail pulls off by itself. This next part always confuses me when I am on horseback, because it takes me along side Rollaway Rd. a little ways then turns me back into the woods, then right back to Rollaway Rd. again, this time crossing it, going a little ways, and then crossing another paved road. Before I took the time to sit down and study the map,

I thought I should have been across three counties. All I did was snake along Rollaway Rd, then cross it before the party store, go behind the party store, cross M-65 and then see nothing but a path winding through the woods for miles. I finally realized that the trail was taking me parallel to River Road about a mile and half south of it. Because it crosses all the mile square roads in the middle, you never get to read those forest posts numbers to know where you are on the map.

Eventually, after about 8 miles of this, the trail crosses a well traveled paved road called Monument River Rd. About a mile down this road is a monument built honoring the lumbermen. It is located right on some high banks of the AuSable River. The horse trail used to follow along these high banks for about 4 miles in the beginning so the horses could drink at a park out of a fountain, but for some reason unbeknownst to me, it was put where it is today, which makes a long day's ride without a drink for the horse.

About two miles from Monument Rd. is another well traveled paved road. This is River Rd. It leads into OsCoda. At this point you are about 6 miles from Old Orchard Park, a township camping place 10 miles from Lake Huron. (Old Orchard Park had a section of it that could be used for horse camping, but in 1995 things changed. As of the printing of this book, there isn't a designated place for horses to camp in this area.) The trail crosses River Rd. and follows parellel to River Rd. about 5 miles. It is the same type of forest that you've ridden through all day. Just before Old Orchard Park the trail crosses River Rd. again and takes you by pathway and along some roads into the township park on the shore of Lake Huron. I'm not sure if you can get to the shore without going through a gate, which is sometimes locked, or if things have changed and you can get to the shore anytime you might arrive there. The park was hearing complaints from non-horse people about the droppings left in the parking area. The stuff us horse people take for granted as part of our sport, is not as welcome to the non-horse loving world.

I wish I could have been more explicit about this part of the trail, but it has been 4 years since I have ridden it. It is a trail that gets you from the lake to a camp and as all trails go, some are very scenic and others are plain. This part is beautiful, but plain!

Oscoda - - Lake Huron

Oscoda - - Lake Huron

Luzerne Bridge

PART THREE

Seven Horse Races Across Michigan
from Oscoda to Empire
1985 - 1991

SHORE TO SHORE 250 MILE RACE OF 1985

Back in the early 1980's I was doing a lot of endurance riding. Fifty miles in one day got to be a piece of cake. I wanted a bigger test. How could I ever tell if I was as tough as the pioneers of the great exodus out west. I had also ridden with the Michigan Trail Riders since 1967 and when on those cross Michigan trips I found I wanted to ride forever. Many times, at campfires, the idea of riding past one camp and going on to the next, making a fifty mile ride per day instead of the usual twenty-five, was the subject of discussion. No one ever seemed to follow through on it though.

The distance riding group we belonged to covered the entire United States and Canada. We would bring up the idea of riding from point to point at fifty miles per day over a certain number of days and people would get excited, but the big question was where could it be done.

Michigan was the perfect state. The Michigan Shore to Shore Trail was already established, thanks to a few Traverse City horseback riding adventurers who created it in the early 1960's. The romance of starting with your feet in a big body of water (Lake Huron) and riding to another big body of water (Lake Michigan) can fool you into imagining you are a pioneer.

The trail is mostly single path with rocks, stumps and logs to beat away at the horse's feet, not to mention the fetlock deep sand in places that can bow a tendon or wear away at energy and bring on muscle fatigue.

The Indian would not pose the problems to us that our forefathers encountered, nor would our wooden wagon wheels need constant greasing with buffalo fat. Our diet would be quite different from the pioneers, what with the invention of coolers and the availability of stores who sell ice, but the imagination has a way of discounting the modern conveniences so that today's person can still feel a sense of accomplishment over and above his fellowmen, if he could just endure this 250 mile adventure.

The endurance riders in the west have had the opportunity for 3 years to try this type of ride when they re-ride the old pony express trail across Utah and Nevada. There is also a multi-day ride from Carson City, Nevada, across the Sierras to San Francisco, Calif. that takes five days. The timing was perfect - the people in the east and midwest were looking for a multi-day challenge.

In the cold winter months of 1984 the challenge went out to the endurance riding populace of the United States via an organization called the American Endurance Ride Conference. A monthly magazine is published keeping these people in touch with new rules and a listing of all the rides in the U.S. and Canada. Special permission had to be sought from the board of directors for this length of ride as most rides are only 50 to 100 miles in one day. Their final conclusion was to accept the fact that we wanted to ride 50 miles a day for 5 days, but they would not accept the total mileage as 250 miles. They did not have any rules set up for points for that length of ride. They would count their points as five single fifty mile rides.

As with any new idea, there are always skeptics, but the Great Lakes Distance Riding Association (centered around Michigan) decided to give the ride their full acceptance. Roger and I took on the responsibility of putting on the ride. I wanted to ride it so I took on the jobs that could be done getting the ride in order and seeing to the prizes. Roger would take over as manager at the ride. We set the dates for the Labor Day weekend of 1985.

I had two friends who would ride with me all summer to get the horses in condition for the big run. Pam Blandin, who boarded her horse at my house, and Joy Plamondon, who was raised in Leland but now lived in Florida. She would come every summer and visit her father bringing her horse with her. The conditioning of horses and riders started in March of 1985 on horses who had already run endurance in 1984 and had been previously ridden in the years up until then. This is not an endeavor for the heavily muscled horse or a box stall horse. The horse has to have been athletically stressed and conditioned from birth. Besides this kind of horse, it takes lot of horsemanship to cover the trail without any problems, fit enough to turn around and go back at the end. Tough enough to go all the way to California if need be.

This challenge keeps us riding 3 to 4 times a week, every week encreasing our distance and finding more difficult terrain. This area is perfect - we are lucky. We start out easily with a ten mile walk and trot in March, and by the time the snow melts in April, we can run the woodland trails. There are easy trails with hard packed sand with a little hill here and there to get us started, then onto more hilly, sandy power lines to put the finishing touches on by July.

The pre-planning with the DNR, which involves maps, safety plans, insurance, and many hours of paperwork, kept us inspired. When those were culminated, the inquires about the ride began. We grew more excited as we heard from top endurance riders from Alabama, Penn., Ohio, Wisconsin, Canada, and it sounded like our challenge would be met.

August arrived and the final polishing of the horses had to be done. We drove to Oscoda and followed the Shore to Shore trail from Oscoda to Luzerne in 2 days, then came home to ride the third day, (110 miles in 3 days). Another weekend we rode from Shecks Place to Empire and again rode another day at home. 130 miles in 3 days. We felt we were ready.

Now for last minute details; new shoes, and every nail must be perfect (our farrier was a nervous wreck); tack had to be in good repair; "conastoge wagon" motor tuned up; spare tire full of air; bottle gas tank full of gas and plenty of water containers. Lastly, who would be brave enough to watch the ranch and feed 40 horses while we're both gone for a whole week? My unsuspecting nephew - he's fearless. What had we forgotten?

Out in Massachusetts, Dr. Rae Mayer, DVM, our vet, was making her final arrangements to leave her job for a week and travel with us to judge our horsemanship and ensure the safety of the horses. Rae worked on endurance rides while attending MSU and the idea of a race across Michigan intrigued her. She said she would come to Michigan to vet it for us if we could ever get it worked out. We would be checked by her every 15 miles with a final thorough vet check each evening, assuring us that our horses were holding up and could take another 50 miles, or warning us of straining tendons or fatigue and suggesting a rest.

The Monday before Labor Day arrives and finds us very excited. Today we haul our horses to Oscoda to a park called Old Orchard Park on the AuSable River. There is some last minute checking to do on the the trail that has to be done and police to contact in town.

The riders and their rigs arrive on Tuesday. Commaraderie is overflowing and the excitement is high. Joe Long, from Alabama, President of the American Endurance Ride Conference; Earl Baxter, Canada, AERC Director, brings a semi-tractor with his big cattle trailer. It will be horse trailer and camper for the week. Earl's wife, Leslie Bond, plans to ride part of the way. Two teenagers, Cory McAllister and Lisa Leeman also come along to ride. Leslie also brings her very British speaking father for their camp cook and pit crew; Marv Nichols, a veteran endurance rider and his teenage daughter, Linda, sign up; Joe Yogus, Michigan's oldest and toughest endurance rider; Kathy Walton, Michigan toughest female endurance rider. Kathy and Joe have been waiting to try this length of ride for years.

The competitive riders are Pam Blandin, Joy Plamondon, Sue Sanborn, riding one of Joy's horses from Lake Leelanau, Sue Herrick and daughter Vicki (age 11) and Jan Kennedy from Merritt, Michigan with her champion Appaloosa mare,

205

and of course myself. All the horses looked in shape to pass the test.

Horses have to be "vetted in" to make sure every horse is well and not lame. There will be 2 kinds of ride: an all out race with times accumulative every day with the same horse and rider - the team having the least time when they run into Lake Michigan will be declared the winner; the second kind of ride is to determine the horse that finishes in best condition that has been ridden by the same rider with time a small factor. The first kind of ride is called an endurance race and the second kind is a competitive trail ride. There are other alternatives like; one person - two horses - taking turns on the horses, or if your horse gets tired you can let him rest a couple of days and ride another day later in the week. Thusly, fifteen people and horses start the big ride.

Tues. Aug. 27, 1985, we try to turn in early (11PM?) because we have to get up at 4 AM to haul the horses 10 miles into the lake shore in Oscoda. Departure time is 6 AM. At 4 AM we hear rain on the "conastoga camper" roof. I jump up to put a waterproof horse blanket on my horse - can't let him get a chill and stiffen up those muscles. All this noise wakes up my husband, who is never mustered by anything and he complains that he can't sleep. Could it be a little excitement has rubbed off onto our ride manager and caravan leader?

5:30 AM. It's pouring rain so the horses are hustled into their trailers with the blankets still on them. Picket lines are pulled down by wet hands and flashlights. Rigs are lined up —Wait — where is Marv Nichols, a seasoned rider from Ohio — no one has seen him this morning; is he awake yet? Windshield wipers are clicking back and forth full speed while someone runs to get him and I sit there hypnotized by them. I remember my studies of wagon trains and I imagine we are at St. Louis hooking up our oxen in the pouring rain, and I wonder how this one will work. Will we end up having one conflict after another, like the Donner Party, who left St. Louis with their wagons full of wealth, all very intelligent people, 88 strong, who would up hassling over every incident, making the whole trip miserable for everyone. In the case of the Donner Party, half of them starved 80 miles from their destination. (Authors note: if you ever get a chance to read about the Donner Wagon Train you will be greatly broadened in your studies of American History and human psycology. If you get to Reno - be sure to visit the museum at Donner Pass.)

We all entered this ride knowing that each day we would grow more tired and less forgiving. We thought of signing a statement that anything said on this trail ride should be wiped immediately from each other's minds.

The rigs start to move. I'm assuming someone found Marv. When we arrive at the beach park the rain has let up to a heavy mist. Horses are being hastily saddled because we must start the ride in 20 minutes. I never saddle hastily so consequently, I am one of the last ones to get to the shore line.

The early morning sun is trying to burn through the fog. Fog horns blow, seagulls conmplain, the waves slap the shore and horses refuse to enter the water. A couple have to be led in by the rider's pit crew. Everyone is finally in the water.

Pictures are taken and it's 7 AM. We're off! A policeman stops traffic at the 4 lane highway - we look impressive - like the cavalry, trot, trot, trot!

We ride the mile through Oscoda together and then the 8 endurance riders move on ahead of us. I plan to ride this like the tortoise and the hare; 250 miles can wear on a horse and I want to have a strong horse at the end. I love my horse - I raised him from a baby. He's ten now and I want him sound at 25.

The ten miles to our first vet check is over a two-track, sandy, with even ground. We move right along at 10 to 12 miles per hour. A mist of fog keeps us cool.

At the first vet check everybody is fine, all ride on. Now the trail turns into a single path, winding through the trees, over stumps and logs with an occasional glimpse of the beautiful AuSable River. The trees are mostly Jackpine and Scrub Oak and the little stumps created in swathing out the trail can be very hazardous to a horse if he either steps directly on one or trips over one. Sure don't need any leg or feet problems at this stage of the game. The front rider in our group of seven is responsible for calling out when one is sighted in the trail. It becomes a song as we trot along, each person singing out in his note "stump on the right, stump on the left, or stump in the middle". Take it from a person with a sensitive ear - our choir left a lot to be desired - but it kept up the morale throughout the day's ride.

The endurance horses have to come back down the trail five miles because the AERC rules say each day's ride must be a legal 50 miles. Because of this we have a chance to meet them, on their way back to put their numbers in a pail, and we know how they are doing. We get to stay in camp (South Branch) when we arrive because the competitive rules say from shore to shore, and we feel really smart because we vet in ahead of the endurance horses. So what's a measly 10 miles. 50 down and 200 to go!

Tuesday evening, along about supper time, the rumbling, snorting, and kicking of horses is heard on the far side of Jan Kennedy's horse trailer. We all hurry over only to find at least 30 yellow-jackets fastened onto both the horses, stinging them, and no way to enter into the frightened horses to release them from the trailer. Finally, Joe Long's pit girl, Nancy, enters the trailer and unties them while other people scurry to catch them again. Gerrie Rem receives at least 3 bee stings on her arm and Vicki Herrick gets it on her ear. Sue Herrick - Vicki's mother - was on hwe way back to the previous camp where she had left her rig. She had temporarily tied them to Jan's trailer not realizing there was a yellow-jackets nest in the ground next to her horses.

Both horses are washed with cold water, while the vet tries to get some of the stingers out. Later, a poultice is applied. The smaller horse received some mean kicks from the larger horse and has to be treated for stress. She is uncomfortable all night so Sue stays up with her. In the morning it is decided that the smaller horse should not be ridden today. We assure Vicki - age 11 - that if her horse gets well and she can ride it 4 days out of the 5 we will still give her her prize for completion (a jacket with the logo of the Shore to Shore 250 on the back) and her mileage for her yearend points. She is riding in her own junior division so competition is no problem.

Thurs. morning it is decided that the competitive horses will leave 1/2 hour earlier since we are moving slower and this will make it easier to keep the vet with all of the horses all day. Again, in a mist, we leave camp toward the west, following the AuSable river toward the camp called McKinley, and after lunch break (1 hour) we will move on to Luzerne camp.

The South Branch to McKinley trail is the most beautiful and the most hazardous. There are hills, gullies, deep sand filled with rocks, at least 19 bridges of various construction from very safe, although slippery, to partly rotted and dangerous. The scenery is very wild as we follow the river and we come across an immature eagle, wild turkeys and deer. The 6 or 7 miles of moguls remind us that we are in the age of machines and our backs get tired from the up and down of them.

At the first vet check, while we are peacefully watering our horses in the river, under the 4001 Bridge, a canoe comes floating around the bend and scares one of the horses, causing the rider, Sue Sanborn, to fall into the water onto her elbow. This results in a bruised elbow and very wet clothing. Luckily her rig is here, as was the practice throughout the week, which allows her to change into dry clothes. Riding in wet clothes can cause blisters.

We travel onward to the vet check at McKinley, where we will get an hour break. We can always tell when a vet stop is coming because it will start to rain. No matter - we have rain gear tied on the saddles. The pit crews put light blankets on the rump muscles of the horses to keep them warm. If those big muscles get cold, they get stiff and tight.

When the vet check over, the rain lets up, and we continue on our way to Luzerne. The history of the late 1800's and early 1900's unfolds before us now, as we ride old railroad beds. We discuss how it was to use horses and shovels to move all that dirt and build all the necessary roads to get the big trees out of the woods to the rivers. Chicago and Detroit were built from trees from these woods. How many men and horses died and are buried underneath us. If you listen you can hear the ghosts.

Onward we go, over stumps and logs, through some hardwoods today with the big wet leaves overhead like umbrellas keeping our horses cool. Boredom is setting in and my lazy horse needs urging forward. Suddenly he spots a shiny car hood about 100 feet off the trail in the woods. He decides to play it to the hilt, (someone told him bears were bright red and shiny) so I, by now sick of pushing him along, let the devil get ahold of me and I start to whoop and holler to make him think that I am afraid also. He takes off in a springy trot, clearing logs the heighth he tripped over before, and we run the last 4 miles to the vet check in no time. Somehow he knew I had used that shy against him because he never pretended to be as frightened the rest of the ride.

As we near Luzerne camp we encounter the big 1/4 mile long bridge built across a swamp with 2 streams. This bridge is very slippery and some of the boards are starting to rot. The MTRA has nailed snowmobile rubber treads on most of it. We decide to lead here and walk cautiously. Nevertheless, one of the boards gives away and Sue Sanborn's horse falls through. His hindquarters slip into the hole also and it looks like a broken leg about to happen. The horse manages to lurch out of the hole to nearly fall over the side into the river, but somehow manages to regain his balance. He is very sore so we have to walk the 3 remaining miles to camp whense it decides to pour. Joy is very worried about her favorite endurance horse.

When we arrive in camp the rain is falling in torrents. Some smart aleck Englishman from Canada asks us if we've been riding in the rain. We say, "No, we've been skinny dipping off the bridge in the swamp." British humor - we grew to love it that week.

That night our vet check is done in a downpour in Luzerne camp which is normally one of the driest camps on the trail. The bridge accident horse will not be ridden on tomorrow as his front leg is very sore. The Vet feels no real damage, but it will take lots of tincture of time to let the horse heal himself.

It is announced that the competitive riders will leave 1 hour before the endurance riders on Friday since we moved so slowly today. It did take us 11 hours on that trek, but we had to be very cautious because of the footing.

Of the original 8 endurance horses who started, 4 will start out on Friday; two are being rested because of lamenessand 2 riders decided to take a day off to rest. They were gaining 2 hours a day on the competitive horses, but we were being especially cautious. We still have our original 7 horses because the bee stung horses are again able to be ridden.

Friday AM, we leave as soon as we can see the trail. It is misty, but we are hopeful when we get out onto the road and see patches of blue sky. Today's trail is easier, mostly a single path through the woods to Smith Bridge for a vet check and the same to 4 Mile camp, with only the last 4 miles deep sand. Here we are lucky that we have had so much rain because there is no dust and we can ride in a group. This group riding helps us keep up our "humorous" morale.

We are not too far behind the endurance riders as they are just leaving their noon break when we arrive. It is sure nice to see those rigs at every stop with blankets for the horses and food the both. We each have different theories on what to feed a working horse. I give mine all the grain he wants plus hay, which really only amounts to 2 - 3 lbs. of grain. The electrolytes are the most important at every 2 hour interval. Our horses are not sweating a whole lot, but it is cool so how can you tell how much evaporates. I always ride more slowly after noon break to help my horse digest his food and rewarm his muscles.

The trail from 4 Mile camp to Goose Creek on the Manistee River, is a long dry run through sand and woods. Part of it is through an army military zone and we are warned to stay on the trail for fear of stepping on a dud bomb. This helps our imaginations to go crazy and the time passes quickly. Our rigs meet us at M-72 for a vet check and water. One of the bee stung horses, owned by Sue Herrick, is getting tired, so Sue pulls back to walk on to camp while daughter decides to ride on with us. Vicki is a good little rider. Her 13hh horse is tough and doesn't always respond to Vicki's horsemanship, but the kid takes the abuse and rids herself of the frustration by saying "Dang it all, Mittie". Many kids and many parents would've given up long ago.

We arrive at Goose Creek one hour and half ahead of the previous day's ride time, to the amazement of everyone. Our comment is - "easier trail today"!

Our second vet joins us today from Whittemore, as we are expecting more people to join us for over the Labor Day weekend. Dr. Tom Dombroski, DVM, had to leave his private practice to help us with our ride. He, also, had worked on our rides in the past and wanted to see people ride 250 miles in 5 days.

The weather cleared and we decided to build a campfire. Sitting around a warm fire allows us a chance to get acquainted with the other riders and pit crews. It gets cold as the sunlight fades and causes a fog to rise off the warm river. The sky fills with stars and a ver bright, full moon. There is no more beautiful camp than Goose Creek. It is story time way into the night. The drivers of the rigs get to tell how they manage to get over the rough back roads to our vet checks. We learn two of the big rigs got hung up in a gully on the powerline short cut. Earl Baxter makes the comment that the cost of the ride is cheap enough but the cost of fixing his rig will cost enough to buy him a trip to California and back. The endurance riders, some of whom have ridden for 30 years, get to re-live old rides and the fellowship of this ride is established.

Sat. 6:30 AM, the five competitive riders are saddled up and ready to go. We have to convince our horses that they want to cross that belly-deep, very cold river. At the call, "Remember the man from snowy river", we lunge the horses into the cold water and we are off.

The trail from Goose Creek to Kalkaska is an easy trail, partly through the woods and then about 6 miles of dirt road riding before you hit Mayhem Swamp. The MTRA has built some very nice bridges over the dangerous places but you must stay on the narrow pathway in between the bridges or you will sink out of sight. This swamp is about 1 mile long and Betty Dykstra, who came to ride the last 100 miles, catches up with us here, and is glad for company for her young horse through here.

Once through, it is onward to Kalkaska camp. We are last again, what with the endurance horses all passing us on the road before the swamp. There are a lot of huge, old, charred stumps in this stretch. This was all lumbered off at one time and later on in time there must have been a forest fire. Most of the trees we are riding through are under 50 years old. Bet these old stumps could tell us some stories.

The noon break is at the river outside of Kalkaska camp. The endurance horses are still there so we aren't too far behind. The horses get their lunch here and so do we.

The trail to Shecks Camp is a sandy, single path with some trail obstacles and my horse is having a problem with his left stifle. When I put him back to the rear of the line he has much more impulsion, since he is afraid of being left alone, so we use that strategy, realizing that most of his pain is a figment of his imagination, attributable to his lazy character.

At Shecks we arrive sooner than expected again with many hours of day light. We hang out our wet horse blankets and clothes, some of which are starting to mildew. Shecks is located on the Boardman River and since it is sunny and warm our horses get to play in the river.

We build a campfire again and people are getting slaphappy. We've only 50 more miles to go. Patches are passed out to the riders and workers and enough praise cannot be said about the trail, the type of ride, and the friendly people. Sunday will be our last leg and the trail is gone over in detail. Two fresh horses will be in an endurance race of their own along with Joe Long who has rested his horse for 2 days. Of the original endurance horses, 4 will be running on Sunday. Of the original competitive 8 horses, 5 will be running Sunday.

Sunday, 6:30 AM, finds the competitive horses being trotted out before the vet. It is a cool day, cloudy, but low humidity, and the horses feel good. We are told to get going and good luck. As we move along, the horses want to move out so we decide to go for it. We make it to Mayfield (6 miles) in 45 minutes, and on through to US 37. Our vet check is behind the fair grounds, but when we get there, in 1 1/2 hours, we do not see our rigs or a vet. We leave a hasty note in the sand and continue our cantering. As we cross US 37 the rigs are just arriving - seems they had to take a detour around River Road. We can't stop here so we just keep trotting right through Grawn and onward to Mud Lake. Dr. Dombroski meets us at US 31 and asks if we have any problems - we say no - and he allows us to keep going.

It takes us 3 hours to go 25 miles and we are ahead of the fresh endurance horses.

Our horses vet in good at Mud Lake and after an hour break we're off and running again. The 3 endurance riders arrive halfway through our break and they have never seen competitive horses move like that. Most competitive trail rides are not permitted to go over 4 miles per hour where they come from (Alabama, Penn. Ohio, and Canada). We explain to them that we can choose our pace but that we are going to be placed in the order or our condition, with time being a small element of the score.

The trail west of Mud Lake is easy riding the first half of the way to Gerry Lake, so we make good time again. We do have to slow down in the deep sandy places. The fresh endurance horses pass us halfway to Gerry Lake, but we feel good to have stayed up front so long.

At the vet check at Gerry Lake we all look good. We hear that the endurance horses made it to the end (6 miles from here) in 19 minutes. We know we aren't going to go anywhere near that fast. After you've ridden 242 miles and your horse is still sound, it is best not to do anything stupid, so we ride at an easy 6 mph to the finish.

We all trot in sound at the end and with great jubilation, recover to way below the parameters in 10 minutes and venture onward along the road the last two miles to the actual shore of Lake Michigan in the town of Empire.

When we ride through town, people look at us like any other person riding a horse through their town. They have no way of knowing about the lump in our throats nor do they notice the tears that keep leaking down our cheeks. They do not realize how exhilerated we feel having covered 250 miles in 5 days using the actual riding time of 39 hours. Our endurance horses did even better by using up only 30 hours to cover the distance.

The shore of Lake Michigan is very rough and our horses do not want to enter - but they must do this one last feat to make the trip complete. Some back in, some are led in, but all get their feet wet.

The next step is to load into trailers and go back 8 miles to Gerry Lake, our final campsite for judging and awards. The challenge was met and conquered. We can relax now.

Everyone who finished receives a jacket with the ride logo on the back. Other prizes are patches, chevrons of mileage, specially monogramed mugs, saddle pads, and leg wraps (specially made), breed awards and handmade wooden framed mirrors.

I am especially not going to list who won what awards because it matters not the final judge's opinion. The feeling inside each and everyone of us that we not only made it all the way, but that we are all very close friends because of it. It is an accomplishment that took team work and without any member of the team it would've been impossible. When we finished we all knew and respected each other from drivers of rigs, P & R people, vets, vet secretaries, pit crews, riders and horses.

This ride is a chance for the horseman of today to leave the fast life of the city and go back to nature. His challenges are the same as the wagon trains and pioneers only of a different era. His world is small and everyone in it must communicate and work together. The thing we discovered was he can also laugh and live together. We have great hope for the Shore to Shore 250 in future years.

Endurance riders who made it the full 250 miles: Kathy Walton, Michigan; Joe Yogus, Michigan; Linda Nichols, Ohio; Cory McAllister, Canada;

Competitive: Pam Blandin, Michigan; Joy Plamondon, Florida; Jan Kennedy, Michigan; Vicki Herrick, Michigan; and, Rhoda Ritter, Michigan.

Joe Yogus

Dr. Tom Dombroski, D.V.M.

Dr. Rae Mayer, D.V.M.

Ray Mayer, Bruce and Marlene Birr

endurance has to be able to run beside his horse part of the way. There are weight divisions in the American Endurance Ride Organizations that give the larger person a chance to compete against people of the same weight. At our special race across Michigan, the veterinary-judges figured time and weight in as a factor. But, no matter how you figure it, you can't put a 100 pound person and a 200 pound person on a 1000 pound horse and expect the horse to carry each person at the same speed and distance. If you study the charts on the next few pages you will see how weight influenced time.

Our two veterinary judges came year after year. Dr. Rae Mayer married Bruce Birr, who acted as her secretary and kept track of statistics, who I thank for making this chapter possible. In a couple of years Marlene was born and then Rae's father started coming along to help with the baby. Dr. Tom Dombroski, from Whittemore, MI, would take a weeks vacation from his private practice to share in the judging. Both veterinarians spent a lot of time helping people with their horses so they could complete the whole distance. Within two days they were on a first name basis with everyone and made many lasting friends.

The first two years we ran the race (1985 & 1986), there were two different kinds of judging criteria. One was a competitive ride where the horse is judged at the end of the ride on his ability to turn around and go another 250 miles. The other was a horse race where the time was accumulated daily, and the horse and rider team with the least amount of time was declared the winner. The coveted award in this kind of race is the best condition and that is determined the same way as it is for the competitive horse.

As you can see by the chart below, we had very few contenders. Joe Yogus rode about the same speed as Kathie Walton and their horses were both in good shape, but because Joe weighed about 75 pounds more than Kathie, his horse was given those handicap points when it came to judging for best condition, which is only fair because Joe's horse did work harder. Joe Long was a lean fellow, so on the days he did ride, he could go faster than Kathie and use his time points for best condition. But you can see who perservered and won the potatoes and the steak. The other finishers were Joe Yogus, (at the time about 63 years old), and the two teenagers: Cory McAlister and Linda Nichols. I believe Earl made it every day, but he did not meet the criteria of one horse-one rider.

Joy Plamondon, Pam Blandin, Jan Mills-Kennedy and I, all completed our competitive ride in good shape. We rode pretty much together and at the same speed. Some days Jan would ride with other people and some with us. My lazy horse Rawhides Apoppin took the best condition award. I learned not to ride a lazy horse because I had to work too hard to keep him going. If I tried to hold him back while the group went on ahead, he would canter in place, so I knew he wasn't tired. He just didn't care to work hard. The two best rides I had were on his sister, Marbisir, who was all business.

215

SIX MORE RACES ACROSS MICHIGAN

The first race proved it could be done. We put the race on for six more years before giving in to the fact that, we would never be able to cover expenses. Other people were trying the multi-day rides out west and were discovering the same truths. There were just not enough people in the sport to keep it going. To run a horse 250 miles in five days means total dedication for at least six months and lots of money. Knowledge and time also enter into the complete picture.

The people who did come to Michigan to try their skills were not disappointed in our beautiful state and our trail, especially those that slowed down enough to see it. No matter how many seemed to start, only 50% of them completed. Many took advantage of the fact that each ride was a single 50 mile in it's entirety. That made it easy for them, but especially hard for anyone trying to ride all the way. Some people brought two horses and switched every other day, giving the other horse a rest. Some people rode only every other day, allowing their horse to rest on the off day. The poor guy trying to make it all the way had a hard time keeping track of who was ahead of him time wise. The total riding time was cut from 31 hours, 44 minutes the first year, to 22 hours, 8 minutes in 1989.

Weight definitely entered into the success of the rider and horse. The criteria for best condition is judged on pulse and respiration recoveries, plus dehydration, lesions, swellings, fatigue, muscle soreness, time, and any signs of lameness plus the weight factor. Any person over 175 pounds who wants to ride

216

1985

Date	Starters	Finishers	Winner	Time	B.C.
8/28/85	7C, 8E	7C, 8E	Joe Long	6:23	Joe Long
8/29/85	5C, 7E	5C, 7E	Joe Yogus	6:52	Joe Yogus
8/30/85	6C, 7E	6C, 6E	Walt Allen	6:16	Joe Yogus
8/31/85	6C, 6E	6C, 6E	Leslie Bond	6:17	Cory McCallister
9/1/85	6C, 9E	6C, 9E	Walt Allen	3:32	Joe Long
Complete 250 mile race	7C, 8E	4C, 5E	Kathie Walton	31:44	Kathie Walton
			Jan (C)	37:31	Rhoda (C)

The fall of 1986 brought more people, now that they found out it could be done. I will give you the names of the people who entered, but I have no way of knowing who intended to ride the complete distance or who only signed up for the daily rides. The Michigan entries were: Kathy Taylor, Judy Schlink, Karen Skuratowicz, Pat Sager, Craig Barsuhn, Carol Hawkins, JoBeth, Bridleman, Nick Mamula, Myra Fleming, and Joe Yogus for endurance. Entries from other states included: Joanne Hanson, MO; Susan Philpot, KY; Bari Farcus, PA; Peg Blair, PA; Annette Taschner, PA; Joe Long, AL; Bill Wilson, KY; Walt Allen, PA; Jill Claire, PA; Paul Bauer, OH; John Philpot, KY; Carrie Smith, OH; Tom Luckett, IN; Trilby Pederson, CA; and Les Carr, CA. The entries for competitive were all from Michigan. They were: Mary Ann Smith, Jan Mills Kennedy, Joy Plamondon, (lived most of the time in Florida but lived summers in MI), and Rhoda Ritter.

It was interesting how each played his strategy. Joy and I were going to ride about the same pace we had the year before although we each were riding different horses. Jan was riding her old faithful appaloosa. Joe Long and Walt Allen were old sparing buddies so they really pushed the first couple of days and paid for it by over riding their horses and had to let them rest for two days. Tom Luckett and Bill Wilson arrived on the third day so they had fresh horses. They must have been good at following a trail, because there were places where they had to search for the trail markers. But they did and they made good time.

Another interesting situation that took place during this years ride was the points war between Trilby Pederson, and Les Carr. The AERC organization counted points for the year-end champion by adding up all the miles a person rode that particular calendar year. They each had over 5000 miles and they were fierce competitors. Les leased a horse to ride three days. He flew into Detroit, arrived at the beginning of our ride, climbed on his horse, rode for three days, and flew to another ride. Trilby had her horses hauled to the ride and flew in and out the same way - only separately. These two people were good friends, but they were also out to prove who was the toughest. Neither of them were spring chickens, both were in their mid fifties.

The people who took up the challenge for the complete distance rode steady and it paid off. Those people were Susan Philpot, KY; Karen Skuratowicz, MI; Judy Schlink, MI; Pat Sager, MI and Jill Claire, PA. The competitive riders who made it in good shape were Jan Mills-Kennedy winning the trophy, with Joy taking second. I disqualified myself from the awards because I felt I knew the trail too well.   One exciting thing happened to a horse at Kalkaska Camp for the noon break and vet check. The rider had loosened up the girth, but left the saddle on. When she took it up to have it checked, the vet asked for a trot in hand. The saddle slipped and slid underneath the horses belly. The horse took off running and bucking with people jumping this way and that to get out of the way. Finally, Dr. Rae Mayer saw her chance to grab the reins and steady the horse. Others then jumped in to untie the girth and remove the saddle.

1986

Date	Starters	Finishers	Winners	Time	B.C.
8/27/86	18	18	Joe Long AL	4:34	Carol Hawkins, MI
8/28/86	15	13	Walt Allen, PA	5:32	Joe Yogus, MI
8/29/86	14	14	Tom Luckett, KY	5:21	Bill Wilson, KY
8/30/86	11	11	Tom Luckett, KY	5:31	Bill Wilson, KY
8/31/86	9	9	Tom Luckett, KY	6:20	Bill Wilson, KY
Complete 250 mile race	4C, 13E	3C, 5E	Susan Philpot, KY	33:24	Susan Philpot, KY Jan (C)

August of 1987 saw more people sign up for the entire race. That year 18 hoped to make it all the way across. Even though we did have some good down pours, the weather was not as rainy as past years. The competitive rides were discontinued, so now everyone rode the race. Entrees from Michigan were: Jan Mills-Kennedy on old faithful, Rugged's Lacy B; Judy Schlink, riding her old faithful Ka-Barrz; Janice Ascione, on Pizzaz, the horse Judy had ridden across the previous year, now owned by Janice; Ron Ascione; Charlotte Richards - DeRidder; Peggy Gobert; Jamie Gobert; Mary Selleck; Don Edwards; Rhoda Ritter, on a white Arab gelding given me by a friend, named Gaylison; Joy Plamondon, on her old faithful, N.D. Diahmond; Heather Pence; Alger Moeller; Joe Yogus, on his old faithful, Magic Carima; Bruce Birr; Vicki Herrick; Christopher Smith; Tammy Wachal; Cindy Davey; and Myra Fleming. Out of state entrees were; Susan Stormer, PA; Gail Rampke, IN; Peter Franklin, OH; Jean Robson, OH; Joe Long, his old faithful Kahlil Khai, AL; James Dailey, AL; Barbara Dailey, AL; Carol Beckner, IN; Edie Booth, TX; Vonita Bowers, TX; Jody Graham, AL; Kathy Kissick, TN; Joe Dell, PA; and Helen Hopkins, PA. Most of these people are riding horses they have ridden many miles in the past. By the time a person spends the time it takes to get a horse in shape to run 250 miles in five days, the human has gained a lot of respect from the horse. The horse that most people rode were of the Arabian breed, although a lean appaloosa did a fine job also. Two Morgans were entered in that year's race.

The weather was cool with some rain. I remember being at the shore of Lake Huron waiting at the water's edge while various horses were being ridden into the water to make their ride legal. Some of the horses wouldn't go into the water and would rear back and end up being led by someone on the ground. Jean Robson's horse she had raised from a baby (1/2 Arab - 1/2 Appy) decided to buck Jean off. Jean took it in stride, saying now that the mare had done that she would feel better and give her a better ride. I will mention that Jean had a million miles of riding on her and she was a good rider, but in endurance riding the stirrups are kept long and this position does not allow for the person to slide down into the saddle for a good seat. It makes it easy for the rider to stand in the stirrups and balance his weight up over the horse's back allowing the horse to move without the hindrance of the rider. If you are leaning a little too far forward when a horse misbehaves or trips, you will be top heavy and fall forward. You can see by the chart below that Jean must have been right about the mood of her horse because she won two races. I do believe she backed off because her horse was showing signs of getting tired. It's hard to do when you are so close to your goal, but that's what makes a champion. It also allows you to keep your horse sound so you can feed it for 30 years.

I remember Helen Hopkin's horse faintly. He was built like a giraffe with those big long front legs and a withers that was high and carried her up over the center of gravity. She was a tall, lean lady and stayed right with him.

I was always amazed at the people who rode the trail faster than I did. I knew there were places that I would not risk running my horse for fear of getting a bruised hoof or a pulled tendon. There are stumps, rocks, deep sand, and mud that can catch a horse just right and lay him up. Maybe the faster horses had that element of luck that goes along with winning.

I must say this group was the most fun of all the rides. Joe Long brought some friends along (Kathy Kissick, Barb and Jim Daily) who were ready to laugh and play games on the trail that kept people wondering what would be next. They made up a little song about the trail and sang it at the Shecks campfire. Joe Long and Kathy Kissick ended up with the same time so they both got second place awards. Barb Daily won the best condition award, so you see they weren't fooling around, while they were fooling around!

1987

Date	Starters	Finishers	Winners	Time	B.C.
8/16/87	26	24	Jean Robson, OH	5:16	
8/17/87	25	21	Judy Schlink, MI	6:00	Joe Yogus
8/18/87	19	13	Helen Hopkins, PA	5:41	
8/19/87	18	17	Jean Robson, OH	4:48	Peter Franklin
8/20/87	16	15	Myra Fleming, MI	5:10	
Complete 250 mile race	18	7	Helen Hopkins, PA	28:09	Barb Daily, AL

The shore to shore race of 1988 saw fewer riders than 1987. We were so in hopes that it would grow and pay the expenses. This was also a much more serious group than the previous year. If you can just get a couple of clowns in the group, it makes it easier to find humor when you get tired. These 1988 riders had a mission and there wasn't any place for foolishness.

The people who signed up from Michigan were: Pat Sager, Susan Stott, Myra Fleming, Karen Skuratowicz, Don Edwards, Rhoda Ritter, on Marbisir who finished the ride in 1986; Joe Yogus, on Magic Carima; Thomas Johnson, on an appy gelding named Caboo; and Charlotte DeRidder. Out of stater's were; Helen Hopkins, back to do it again with same gelding; Wade Scott, MN; Joe Dell, PA; Helen Nelson, IL; Connie Gray, WI; Kim Kingsley, NB, on a spanish mustang stallion; Michael Mocilan, IL; Jody Graham, AL; David Gorski, WI; Susan Stormer, PA; Earl Baxter, Canada; Steven Bond, Canada; Maggy Price, PA, vice president of AERC; Bill Wilson, IN; Bonnie Twardowski, PA; Patti Karas, WI; and Norm Cooper, WI.

Earl Baxter came back to make it all the way on one horse, and if you look at the chart below, he did and won some best condition awards along with his goal. He is a big man and has to do a lot of running beside his horse to keep his horse from getting overtired. Tom Johnson made his appearance this year. He was a young man studying pre-vet so he was pretty keyed in on his horse. His horse was a tall, lean, appy gelding who barely knew Tom was on his back. He had enough energy to run, but enough sense to let it all down at a vet check. Tom was running against Patti Karas from Wisconsin, Norm Cooper, from Wisconsin, Connie Gray, from Wisconsin, who all were riding two horses, letting one rest a day and riding the other.

Patti Karas and Norm Cooper were no spring chickens, but they had some appy-arab horses that were tough. I remember being at Shecks when about 8 horses rounded the bend together and were racing for the finish line in front of the pump. Patti's horse did something that caused her to end up on the ground and the horse just kept racing in with the rest. Someone caught him and took him back to her, whereupon she took the reins and ran on in with him, enabling her to receive her points for finishing the ride. I asked her if she was hurt. She said, "Only my pride!"

The winner of the complete 250 miles was Tom Johnson who cut 4 hours off Helen's time from the year before. Bonnie Twardowski won best condition. She was just a might smaller than Tom, so she must have had better recovery scores than he. Other people also finishing all 250 miles on a sound horse were: David Gorski, Bill Wilson, Maggie Price, Earl Baxter, Joe Yogus, Rhoda Ritter, Don Edwards, and Wade Scott.

221

1988

Date	Starters	Finishers	Winners	Time	B.C.
8/22/88	23	20	Patti Karas, WI	4:43	David Gorski
8/23/88	18	17	Helen Hopkins	5:26	Earl Baxter, Canada
8/24/88	18	18	Patti Karas, WI	4:06	Patti Karas, WI
8/25/88	15	14	Connie Gray	4:34	Earl Baxter, Canada
8/26/88	19	17	Patti Karas, WI	3:52	Earl Baxyter
Complete 250 mile race	16	10	Tom Johnson, MI	24:08	Bonnie Twardowski PA

The 1989 shore to shore race across Michigan was again held in the last part of August. 13 people signed up to ride all the way, 8 made it. 37 people attended the ride and rode at least one day. Some used more than one horse, and some paid day by day, costing them more and eliminating them from the final judging. A person planning to ride all the way on one horse, had to declare it the very first day. The rest of the riders were riding for AERC points and were of no concern to the five day riders. There were a few people who came back this year to try a different horse or a different strategy. There were daily rider's meetings where daily winners were announced, and the next day's trail was discussed, but, only on the night before the last day's ride, were the accumulated times revealed to the riders. This enabled them to stay awake all night to plan their strategy for the last day's ride. A rider had to place in the first ten across the finish line to get his AERC points for the daily rides. I remember one year how this rule affected a young lad from MN. He was really trying to stay in front of me because he figured he would be in tenth place if he didn't let anyone pass him. Let me say here that everyone paces themselves differently. I know the trail so I can pick my places where I want to make time, and when the going gets rough, I walk. This a great advantage over a first time rider. I finally told him that I was not a member of AERC, or UMECRA, so when we were near the end, I would make sure he crossed in front of me. At that he relaxed and enjoyed the scenery and his ride.

People who signed up from Michigan were: Craig Olsen; Joe Yogus; Thomas Johnson; Jan Mills-Kennedy, Karen Skuratowicz, Kelly Rau, Judy Schlink, and Julie Roe. From other states and Canada: Mike Caudill, KY; Helen Nelson, IL; Judith Schmid, WI; Wendy Maas, WI; Darolyn Butler, TX; CeCi Butler-French, TX; Connie Rawski, Ontario; Rick Nelson, IL; Connie Caudill, KY; Pat Olive, MD; Karleen Vivirito, IL; Sharon Glaski, WI; Sharon Mitchell, IL; Pat French, TX; Norm Cooper, WI; Lynn Allger, IL; Patty Karas, WI; and Carol Steiner, Ontario, Canada.

Carol Steiner had some bad luck the day before the ride started. She and Connie Rawski were keeping their horses together in an electric wire corral. Carol's horse somehow got a puncture in the front leg that caused the horse a lot of pain. The horse was treated, wrapped, iced, walked, run, and coddled. By the third day she was able to be ridden. I remember the big Thoroughbred mare looking like Secretariat, copper chestnut with white stockings. Carol only got to ride her two days. Her camping partner, Connie Rawski did very well. The two women brought their 4 children (one was in diapers but could run around) and two husbands. The husbands moved the rigs, and cared for the children. They did a marvelous job. We did meet the nicest people while we were putting on these rides.

One really nice man (Norm Cooper, 57) got separated from his horse just outside the finish line on the first day. His horse went one way around a tree and Norm went the other. He broke his wrist, but stayed out the week to have it worked on and to help Patti Karas finish the race. He said he only intended to have that wrist fixed once and he wanted to make sure he had the right doctor.

Northern Michigan is not the center of a hub; there are no short cuts across the lakes. People who wanted to haul a horse and camper to our rides usually tried to find someone else to share the expenses. This worked fine if both horses managed to keep going, but in the case of Norm and Patti, and I might say, this was not a rare case, the guy who gets pulled now has to haul his horse from camp to camp, and usually give it special care for the reason it was pulled.

Another thing that made it hard to attend our rides was that a person who wanted to ride it, had to find someone else that would give up at least a week of their busy life to come along and drive the rig from camp to camp. Usually this meant following the caravan all day from vet check to vet check because the roads on the east side of the state are seldom marked. A lot of times these so called "rigs" are big 3/4 ton trucks with gooseneck trailers that are at least 26 feet long allowing for living quarters in them. Maybe you have a friend who is willing to give up a week of their life, but do they know how to drive a truck and trailer?

A little different set of circumstances unfolded as this ride went across the state. We now had a 7 year old child who loved to ride. Her horse just paced himself at about 12 mph and floated along that trail without being hampered by weight. Behind him came the adults. Her mother's horse was very well conditioned to carry an adult, and had little problem keeping up with the child. (There was a rule that any child had to be accompanied by an adult.) Connie Caudill's horse was smaller, but so was Connie, so they could keep up with the child's horse also. Tom Johnson

223

knew how he had paced it the year before, but didn't think he should push the three front runners. He chose to not go for the time award, but hoped he could use his knowledge to get the best condition award. So the contest was up to CeCi, Darolyn, and Connie. Connie was not as experienced at the game as Darolyn, but she hung in there and ended up with two hours less of riding time making her the winner. Tom Johnson was second in time, but won the award he wanted most, the best condition. CeCi was second in best condition. Her horse was in beautiful shape, but she had a severe weight handicap. Connie Rawski was third in best condition, (one of the moms) and Mike Caudill, (a heavyweight rider) was fourth. Connie was fifth, and Darolyn was sixth. Other finishers were: Rick Nelson, Julie Roe, and then there was Wendy Maas, and Helen Nelson who did not enter the 250 race, but entered each ride separately, who were very happy that they had completed the whole distance.

1989

Date	Starters	Finishers	Winners	Time	B.C.
8/21/89	20	18	Craig Olson, MI	4:13	Mike Caudill, KY
8/22/89	21	20	CeCi Butler-French, TX	5:02	Connie Rawski, Canada
8/23/89	17	16	conniue Caudill, KY	4:39	Tom Johnson, MI
8/24/89	22	21	Connie Caudill, KY	4:03	Darolyn Butler, TX
8/25/89	14	11	CeCi Butler-French, TX	4:06	Tom Johnson, MI
Complete 250 mile race		8	Connie Caudill, KY	22:08	Tom Johnson, MI

The 1990 ride was our best year. 34 people lined up at the Lake Michigan shore line. Some were daily riders, and some were 5 day riders, but we made an impressive sight. People from Michigan were: Debbie Olson, Craig Olson, Jan Mills-Kennedy, Karen Skuratowicz, Maryann Barger, Christine Umscheid, Nick Mamula, Myra Fleming, Joe Yogus, and Pat Sager. Out of state entrees were: Bobbie Barber, TX; Lori Windows, IL; Tom Sites, VA; Dorothy Lindell, IN; Daryle Lindell, IN; Connie Caudill, KY; Trilby Pederson, CA; Pat Oliva, MD; Buddy Cirmella, S.C.; Nancy Orth, OH; Mike Caudill, KY; L.G. Neal, PA; Lawton Johnston, S.C.; Trevor Warren, CA; Helen Nelson, IL; Jim Rogan, KY; Les Carr, CA; Geri Brooks, CA; Vivian Stefanchik, OH; Jean Robson, OH; Connie Rawski, Ontario; Pamela Huffstodt, IL; Joy Plamondon, FL; Bill Wilson, IN; Rick Nelson, IL; Norman Cooper, WI; Wendy Maas, WI; Susan Kasemeyer, TN; Lois Bradley, S.C.; Darolyn Butler, TX; CeCi Butler-French, TX; and Rita Bolli, OH.

If you look at the list of the people, you will see many familiar names. Over half of them had ridden the trail before, most of them very experienced riders. Three over 60 years of age: Joe Yogus, Bobbie Barber, and Lawton Johnston. Then there was that little 8 year old girl that loved to run through the woods. Craig Olson was riding a mare he hoped to take to the Race of Champions. Lori Windows brought her appaloosa mule. She warned us if she did not get into a vet check sometime, it would be because her mule had stopped in the trail and refused to go any further.

Connie Rawski, who had done so well the year before, came with high hopes that were shot down the very first day. Her beautiful arab gelding came into the noon vet check a little off in the front. The vets found a stick, about the size of a pencil, sticking into the side of the fetlock under the skin along side the sesamoid bone. They managed to pull it out and it was over two inches long. Although the horse was not real sore on it, it was decided to pull him and treat him. As with all serious contenders, she had entered him in another race in a couple of weeks and wanted him sound, so medicinal treatment was desired. (You cannot run a horse on any kind of drug.) She took him home. Rumor had it that she had more bad luck with him after she got him home.

CeCi, her mother Darolyn, and Connie Caudill set the pace of the ride and held it all week. Everyone else seemed to have set their own goal and held their pace rather than risk being pulled. Trilby Pederson wanted to make it all the way and ride the next week, so she went really slow. She told me the whole trail was like a ride in the park, it was so beautiful. Les Carr brought two more riders with him who hoped to make it all the way so they also rode slow- - about 8 mph. They were Geri Brooks, and Trevor Warren. Pat Sager had urged Lawton Johnston to try it and they were determined that he could, even though he was 66 years old. Norm Cooper, Wendy Maas, Bill Wilson, Pat Oliva, Lois Bradley, Buddy Cirmella, Helen and Rich Nelson, all had new stratedgy and were going to do their best to make it

225

all the way across to Lake Michigan.

No one could catch CeCi and her mother this year. It was a little hairy at the very last vet check at Gerry Lake, just 6 miles from the finish. Darolyn's horse was one pulse beat above parameters when I took it. I immediately backed away and turned her over to Dr. Mayer, saying, "I think you'd better take this one." Pat Oliva was having a problem with her horse's pulse also. The pulse is taken exactly 10 minutes after the horse gets into the check. He has certain numbers he has to come down to in order to go on. They are usually 68 pulse, 68 respiration. If they are not reached in 10 minutes, he gets another 10 minutes, but they have to be down by then, or he does not continue. He is held, cooled down, and hauled to camp. You can imagine how tense everyone (rider and vet) is after riding 244 miles and then face the possibility of not finishing. Both horses were allowed to go on, but the riders had lost precious time. In this case, CeCi could not go on either, because, she, being a junior rider, had to be within one minute of her sponsor- - - Darolyn. All's well that ends well, they say, and CeCi won the race across Michigan in 1990. Connie Caudill was 24 minutes behind CeCi's time of 22:43. She did, however, take the best condition award. Here again remember CeCi loses a point for every 2 pounds she weighs less than her competitors. Even in spite of that, she placed 2nd on best condition. Susan Kasemeyer, a new face to us, but an old hand at endurance riding, placed 3rd in best condition. Next were Bill Wilson, Darolyn Butler, Lois Bradley, Pat Oliva, Lori Windows (the mule rider), Jim Rogan and L.G. Neal. The rest of the 17 finishers were: Pat Sager, Lawton Johnston, Geri Brooks, Les Carr, Trevor Warren, Helen Nelson, and Trilby Pederson

1990

Date	Starters	Finishers	Winners	Time	B.C.
8/20/90	34	29	Craig Olson, MI	4:07	Connie Caudill, KY
8/21/90	32	30	Bobbie Barber, TX	4:31	Darolyn Butler, TX
8/22/90	31	29	Debbie Olson, MI	4:16	Debbie Olson, MI
8/23/90	24	23	CeCi Butler French, TX	4:15	Pamela Huffstot, IL
8/24/90	25	24	Susan Kasemeyer	5:15	CeCi Butler French, TX
Complete 250 miles		17	CeCi Butler French, TX	22:43	Connie Caudill, KY

The 1991 race across Michigan was the straw that broke the camel's back. Besides the Race of Champions, there was an International Endurance race out of Carson City that same summer. We were warned that the riders were spread too thin, and our ride would be the one to suffer. It was too late. The ride schedule had already gone out to the public and people were planning their vacations. We'd just have to take our chances. We did, we lost.

The riders from Michigan were: Joe Yogus, on his old faithful Carima (I will note here that Joe died a few years after riding our ride. He was off by himself, riding his horse and did not come home at dark. He was found by his daughter laying in the woods with his horse grazing close by - cause of death - heart attack.) Valerie Harris, Gene Dake, Pat Sager, Jill Gobert, and Ray Sugzda. Out of staters were: Dorothy Lindell, IN; Peter Franklin, OH; Sandy McDermott, OH; Kate McDermott, OH; Jean Robson, OH; Gail Rampke, IN; Nancy Orth, OH; Lawton Johnston, S.C. now age 67; Lois Bradley, S.C.; Wendy Maas, WI; Mary Chmielewski, OH; Gina Rich, OH; Ted Klopfenstein, IN; Buddy Cirmella, S.C.; and Daryle Lindell, IN.

Wendy Maas had her stratedgy all planned. She headed west toward Lake Michigan on Rushcreek Quasar, a beautiful chestnut gelding. Gene Dake fell in behind and liked her pace so the two rode together the whole ride. They took turns coming across the finish line. Their best condition scores were usually only a couple of points difference daily. But, Wendy only entered each days ride the night before, so she did not qualify for the awards at the end of the ride. She took best condition that fifth day, so can you imagine how the winners would have placed if she had thrown her money on the table the first day and said she was going all the way. As it was, Gene Dake got the steak and potatoes. He also was the first heavyweight person to win the Shore to Shore 250. He took 28 hours and 1 minute to do it. Buddy Cirmella was second in time, then Lois Bradley, Darell Lindell, and Pat Sager. Lawton Johnston rode only 4 days.

The awards given each year were valued at under $50.00, usually something special that signified the ride and logo. Every person who completed the whole distance on a sound horse would get a nylon jacket with a quilted lining, with the name of our ride on the back and a horse being ridden across the state of Michigan. The trail would be lined out, showing each camp. To ride 250 miles in 5 days was a self achievement award and you'd see tears in the eyes of the more sentimental along M-72 as they rode through Empire. The more exuberant danced on the picnic tables back at Gerry Lake.

We met a lot of nice people by putting on the races across Michigan. People we would have never had a chance to know otherwise. When you live with people for 6 days under the stress these people were under you sometimes get to see the sides of people they usually try to keep hidden. But like the wagon trains that traveled together out west, little fuss was made when the tired person let go, and in a little while he would gather himself up again and keep going.

A lot of people were disappointed when we did not schedule our ride for 1992. They loved our trail, and our vets, and they planned all year to come to Michigan. They also understood when expenses can't be made, then things have to be sacrificed. The other rides out west were having the same problems. The Race of Champions would throw in the towel in only a couple of years.

1991

Date	Starters	Finishers	Winners	Time	B.C.
8/20/90	34	29	Craig Olson, MI	4:07	Connie Caudill, KY
8/21/90	32	30	Bobbie Barber, TX	4:31	Darolyn Butler, KY
8/22/90	31	29	Debbie Olson, MI	4:16	Debbie Olson, MI
8/23/90	24	23	CeCi Butler-French, TX	4:15	Pamela Huffstot, IL
8/24/90	25	24	Susan Kasemeyer, TN	5:15	DeCi Butler-French, TX
Complete 250 mile race		17	DeCi Butler-French, TX	22:43	Connie Caudill, KY

Following are 6 graphs comparing the times it took to cover the same distances on the different years. Weather was not a factor because if it wasn't raining, it was cool. The big determining factors were weight and experience. The people who rode it the fastest had a lot of experience in running 100 mile races in one day. They knew their horses and they knew how to ride. They also knew how to take care of their horses at the end of the day so they could run again the next.

The first ride in 1985 shows us the riders were cautious. Riding 50 miles 5 days in a row was a new test and people wanted to finish. We all found out that the third day was the hardest, then the horses seemed to get stronger. That same phenomenon seemed to prove true every year. The horses weren't exhausted at the end, they could have turned around and gone back. Most of them had lost weight, so how far they could keep going at the pace they were setting would depend on each individual horse. But energy wise, they were not used up.

The fastest times were set when the little girl rode up front. The two horses running with her showed signs of being tired which tells us that weight definitely plays a big part in how fast the horse can go. Those same two horses, moving just a little slower, would have probably felt more energetic at the end. A horse is a herd animal and he will not be left behind, no matter the load.

1991 was again ridden by more cautious people. Most of them were in the heavy weight division of AERC and were used to pacing themselves according to what their horses could do easily. This group was also out to complete the ride, not beat any time records. It is really an interesting study, pitting all the different factors against each other; horses, people, weights, experience, knowledge, weather, and the desire to win. I'm glad I had the chance to be there.

Lake Huron to South Branch + 10		South Branch to Luzerne	
1985	6:23	1985	6:51
1986	6:45	1986	5:32
1987	5:16	1987	6:00
1988	4:43	1988	5:26
1989	4:13	1989	5:02
1990	4:07	1990	4:31
1991	5:38	1991	6:21

Luzerne to Goose Creek		Goose Creek to Shecks	
1985	5:05	1985	6:17
1986	5:21	1986	5:31
1987	5:41	1987	4:48
1988	4:06	1988	4:31
1989	4:39	1989	4:03
1990	4:16	1990	4:15
1991	5:06	1991	5:12

Shecks to Lake Michigan		Lake Huron to Lake Michigan	
1985	3:32	1985	31:44
1986	6:20	1986	32:43
1987	4:32	1987	28:05
1988	3:52	1988	23:28
1989	4:06	1989	22:08
1990	5:15	1990	22:41
1991	5:12	1991	28:01

If Tony and Sally Wilhelm would've gone on home in 1963, instead of stopping to visit Jim Hardy, we may never have had the opportunity to ride across the state of Michigan on horseback. We thank you all; the creators, and the caretakers of the shore to shore Michigan Riding and Hiking Trail.

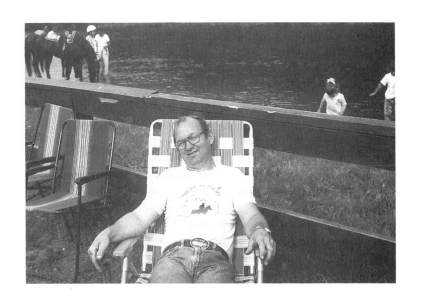

Roger Ritter, Trail Boss

Norm Cooper

In the Water at Empire